NORWAY TRAVEL GUIDE 2024

INSIDER TIPS FOR EXPLORING FJORDS, URBAN GEMS, AND OUTDOOR ADVENTURES WITH EXPERT ITINERARIES AND BUDGET-FRIENDLY ADVICE

EIRA LOFTHUS

BASIC AND ADVANCED GUIDE

CONTENTS

INTRODUCTION

Thank you for choosing this guide. I've put a lot of effort into sharing my experiences and gathering extra information to make it as complete as possible. If you find any issues or need more details, please contact me.

For the first, you should visit this country because it's incredibly beautiful and offers experiences you can't find anywhere else. Like deep blue fjords surrounded by towering cliffs, like Geirangerfjord and Nærøyfjord, where you can take a breathtaking cruise, or think about watching the Northern Lights in Tromsø during winter or enjoying the endless daylight of the Midnight Sun in summer. Every year, millions of tourists come here to see these stunning landscapes and engage in outdoor activities. In 2019, around 5 million visitors came, spending an average of 1,200 NOK per day. This place really is as amazing as it looks on social media, with beautiful nature and nice cities that mix old and new.

Norway is covering about 385,207 square kilometers, this country is home to around 5.4 million people. The locals are friendly and respectful, appreciating visitors who show respect for their customs and environment. This mutual respect makes tourists feel welcome and comfortable. The history is rich and fascinating, from the Viking Age, when Norse explorers ventured far and wide, to the discovery of oil in the North Sea in the 1960s, which transformed the economy. Modern cities like Oslo and Bergen show how tradition and innovation coexist, with eco-friendly practices and green spaces. Oslo, the capital, offers cultural treasures like the Viking Ship Museum and the striking architecture of the Oslo Opera House. Bergen, known for its colorful wooden houses and bustling fish market, serves as a gateway to the fjords and provides a charming historical ambiance.

The cultural heritage is equally compelling. The Sami people, the indigenous inhabitants of the Arctic region, offer beautiful experiences like reindeer herding and traditional crafts. You can visit Sami villages like Karasjok to understand their traditions. National holidays, such as Constitution Day on May 17th, feature beautiful parades and traditional costumes. Beyond the cities, the natural landscapes are spectacular. You can hike the trails of Jotunheimen National Park, home to the highest peaks in Northern Europe, or visit the Lofoten Islands, known for their dramatic scenery and quaint fishing villages. Each region has its own unique character and attractions, from the Arctic adventures in Svalbard to the coastal charm of Stavanger, with its famous Preikestolen cliff. Let's go on next chapter and understand more about Norway!

1 NORWAY

The Vikings, those brave warriors and traders who sailed the seas in longships from the late 8th to early 11th centuries. Their raids and settlements spread far and wide, leaving a big impact on the cultures of Europe. You can still see bits of their legacy today in museums and ancient sites all over.

After the Viking Age, there was a period of unification under King Harald Fairhair, who is often credited with being the first king to unite the kingdom. This unity grew stronger over centuries, though it experienced several unions with Denmark and Sweden. The most notable was the Kalmar Union with Denmark and Sweden that began in 1397. The country gained its full independence from Sweden in 1905, marking a new chapter in its history.

The land is like a masterpiece crafted by nature. The fjords, like Geirangerfjord and Nærøyfjord, were carved by glaciers during the last Ice Age and are now filled with clear blue seawater. These fjords are surrounded by tall cliffs and green hillsides, making them perfect for scenic cruises or thrilling hikes. Jotunheimen, home to the highest mountains in Northern Europe, offers trails that wind through breathtaking alpine scenery, perfect for hiking enthusiasts.

The coastline, with jagged edges and thousands of islands, is like a paradise for who love the sea. Fishing, boating, and visiting these coastal are popular activities. The Lofoten Islands, in particular, stand out with their dramatic peaks rising straight from the sea and picturesque fishing villages. This area is also a great spot to experience the Midnight Sun in summer and the Northern Lights in winter.

Culturally, this place is like a mix of old and new influences. The Sami people, who are the indigenous inhabitants of the Arctic region, have a rich cultural heritage that includes reindeer herding, traditional crafts, and a unique language. You can learn about their way of life and traditions in places like the Sami Parliament in Karasjok or by visiting a Sami village.

National holidays and festivals are deeply rooted in traditions. Constitution Day on May 17th is celebrated with parades, traditional costumes called bunads, and various festivities. It's a day filled with pride and joy, reflecting the country's love for freedom and democracy. Traditional music and folk dances are also important cultural expressions, often seen during festivals and events.

The Capital of Norway is Oslo. You can visit the Vigeland Park, which features over 200 sculptures by Gustav Vigeland, or the Royal Palace, where the Norwegian royal family resides. The Viking Ship Museum showcases some of the best-preserved Viking ships and artifacts, giving you a glimpse into the seafaring life of the Vikings.

Bergen, often called the gateway to the fjords, is a charming city with colorful wooden houses in the UNESCO-listed Bryggen area. This historic wharf was once the center of the Hanseatic League's trading empire. Today, it's filled with shops, galleries, and restaurants. The Fløibanen funicular takes you to the top of Mount Fløyen, offering stunning views of the city and the surrounding fjords.

The Lofoten Islands, with their rugged landscapes, are perfect for outdoor adventures. You can hike to secluded beaches, fish in the rich waters, or even surf in the Arctic. These islands are also one of the best places to see the Northern Lights, especially during the winter months when the nights are long and dark.

Trondheim, another beautiful historical city, is a home to the Nidaros Cathedral, the northernmost medieval cathedral in the world. This city, founded by the Viking King Olav Tryggvason in 997, is also known for the cultural scene and lively student population.

For transportation, the Bergen Railway is one of the most scenic train journeys you can take, offering beautiful views of mountains, fjords, and forests. The Hurtigruten coastal ferry service is another excellent way to visit the remote coastal areas, stopping at numerous ports along the way.

Accommodations here cater to all tastes and budgets. You can stay in luxurious hotels with modern amenities, cozy hostels that are not so expensive, or traditional rorbuer cabins in the Lofoten Islands for a rustic experience.

For the food you must try some traditional dishes like rakfisk (fermented fish), brunost (brown cheese), and lutefisk (dried fish treated with lye).

TRAVEL INFORMATION

To apply for a visa, go to a consulate or embassy with the valid passport. You should have the passport valid for at least three months beyond the departure date. You will need two recent passport-sized photos, a completed visa application form, proof of travel insurance covering at least €30,000, a detailed travel itinerary, and proof of sufficient funds, like recent bank statements showing at least €500 for a short stay. The visa application fee is around €80, and it's non-refundable. You have to apply at least three months before you plan to travel.

Norway uses the Norwegian Krone (NOK). Typically, 1 USD equals about 10 NOK, making it easy to convert prices by dividing the NOK amount by ten. For example, if something costs 500 NOK, it's roughly $50.

ATMs are everywhere and accept international debit and credit cards. You may want to inform the bank about your travel plans to avoid any issues. Avoid exchanging money at airports or hotels because of higher fees and less favorable rates. Use banks or official currency exchange offices instead. If you want some local currency when you arrive, exchange a small amount at your local bank before you leave.

Credit and debit cards, especially Visa and MasterCard, are accepted almost everywhere, from restaurants and shops to public transport and tourist attractions.

For managing your money efficiently, try a multi-currency travel card. These cards let you load money in your home currency and convert it to NOK at competitive rates, helping you avoid foreign transaction fees.

2 OSLO

Oslo with about 700,000 people living there and covering 454 square kilometers, it's the largest city around.

Oslo is at the top of the Oslofjord, surrounded by hills and forests. This makes it great for nature lovers. You can take a ferry on the fjord, hike in the nearby Nordmarka forest, or relax in the parks. The scenery is beautiful and adds to the city's charm.

Founded around 1040 by King Harald Hardrada, it became the capital in the early 1300s. A fire in 1624 led King Christian IV to rebuild it near Akershus Fortress and rename it Christiania. It got its original name, Oslo, back in 1925.

The city is known for its mix of old and new buildings. You'll see the old Akershus Fortress next to modern places like the *Oslo Opera House* and the *Barcode Project*. This mix makes Oslo's look unique and very beautiful.

For the first you have to check out the Vigeland Sculpture Park with over 200 sculptures by Gustav Vigeland. The Viking Ship Museum has well-kept Viking ships showing the life of old Norse explorers. Art lovers should visit the Munch Museum to see Edvard Munch's famous painting "The Scream."

Oslo's food is varied. Try traditional dishes like rakfisk (fermented fish) and brunost (brown cheese), or enjoy modern meals at gourmet restaurants.

Mathallen Food Hall is a great place to taste different foods. So you have many options.

ATTRACTIONS

You absolutely have to check out the **Viking Ship Museum** on Bygdøy Peninsula.

This place has some of the best-preserved Viking ships you'll ever see, like the Oseberg, Gokstad, and Tune ships. These ancient ships were used for burials and are filled with treasures that give you a fascinating glimpse into Viking life. You'll see artifacts like tools, textiles, and even a beautifully crafted Viking wagon. The museum is open every day, from 9 AM to 6 PM in the summer and 10 AM to 4 PM in the winter. It costs 120 NOK for adults and 50 NOK for children to get in. To avoid crowds, it's best to visit in the morning. You can get there easily by taking bus number 30 or hopping on a ferry from the City Hall Pier.

Another must is the **Royal Palace**, which is the official residence of the monarch. Built in the early 19th century, the palace is at the end of Karl Johans gate and is surrounded by beautiful gardens. During the summer, from late June to mid-August, you can take guided tours inside. These tours let you see the State Rooms and learn about the palace's history. Tickets are about 135 NOK for adults and 100 NOK for students and seniors. Be sure to catch the Changing of the Guard ceremony at 1:30 PM every day – it's free to watch and really impressive. The palace is easy to reach by tram or bus, and it's near the city center.

Then, you should visit **Vigeland Park**, also known as Frogner Park. It's the world's largest sculpture park made by a single artist, Gustav Vigeland. The park has over 200 sculptures that explore the human experience, from birth to death. It's open all day, every day, and it's free to enter. Early morning or late afternoon is the best time to go to avoid crowds. The park is great for a picnic, a relaxing walk. You can get there with a short tram ride (lines 12 and 15) or bus ride (bus number 20) from the city center.

The **Munch Museum** if you love art is dedicated to Edvard Munch, the artist famous for "The Scream." The museum has a huge collection of his works, including paintings, prints, and drawings. It's open daily from 10 AM to 6 PM, and tickets cost around 160 NOK for adults, with discounts for students and seniors. To get there, you can take the tram or bus to Tøyen, and it's just a short walk from there.

To learn about local life, visit the **Mathallen Food Hall**. It's a great place to try traditional dishes like rakfisk (fermented fish) and brunost (brown cheese), as well as modern Norwegian cuisine. There are lots of different food stalls and shops, so you can sample a bit of everything. The food hall is open from 10 AM to 8 PM, and it's located in the Vulkan area, which you can reach by taking a tram or bus to Grünerløkka.

The **Akershus Fortress** is another fascinating spot. This medieval castle has stood the test of time since the late 13th century. It offers fantastic views over the harbor and the city. You can explore the grounds for free, but if you want to go inside and see the castle's interior and the Norwegian Resistance Museum, there's a small fee. The fortress is open daily from 6 AM to 9 PM, and you can get there easily by walking from the city center or taking a tram or bus.

WHAT TO EAT

Well, when you're in the city and hungry for some amazing food, you've got to start with **Maaemo** at Dronning Eufemias gate 23. This place has three Michelin stars, which means the food is incredible. They use local ingredients to create a tasting menu that costs around 3,000 NOK per person. *It's expensive, but trust me, it's worth every krone.* You need to book your table well in advance because it's super popular. You can get there easily by taking tram lines 13 or 19 to Bjørvika or a bus to Bjørvika Terminal.

For a more laid-back atmosphere, you should visit **Mathallen Food Hall** in the Vulkan area. This place is heaven for food lovers, with all kinds of local and international dishes. *It's the best spot to try traditional foods like rakfisk, which is fermented fish, and brunost, a unique brown cheese.* Mathallen is open from 10 AM to 8 PM Monday to Saturday, and 11 AM to 6 PM on Sundays. It's located at Vulkan 5, and you can get there by taking tram lines 11 or 12 to Schous Plass and walking for about 10 minutes, or by bus lines 34 or 54 to Møllerveien.

If seafood is what you're after, **Fiskeriet Youngstorget** at Youngstorget 2B is the place to go. They serve some of the freshest seafood in town. *You have to try their fish and chips for about 150 NOK or the seafood platter for around 300 NOK.* They also have a fish market where you can buy fresh fish to cook at home. It's best to visit during lunch or early dinner to avoid the busiest times. Fiskeriet is open from 11 AM to 10 PM, Monday to Saturday, and you can get there by taking tram lines 11, 17, or 18 to Brugata and walking for about five minutes, or by bus lines 37, 54, or 74 to Hammersborggata.

If you like coffee, **Tim Wendelboe** at Grüners gate 1 is a must. Known for its world-class coffee, they roast their own beans, making every cup fresh and flavorful. *You should try their espresso or cappuccino with a freshly baked pastry.* The café is open from 8 AM to 6 PM Monday to Friday, and 10 AM to 5 PM on weekends. It's just a short walk from Birkelunden tram stop, which is served by lines 11, 12, and 13, or you can take bus line 30 to Birkelunden.

If you want vegetarian or vegan food, you have to try the **Nordvegan** at Kristian IVs gate 15. This plant-based bistro offers delicious and healthy dishes like vegan lasagna for about 160 NOK or a BBQ jackfruit sandwich for around 140 NOK. *They also have great smoothies and juices.* Nordvegan is open from 11 AM to 8 PM Monday to Saturday, and it's easy to reach by taking tram lines 11, 17, or 18 to Tullinløkka, or by bus lines 31, 37, or 46 to Prof. Aschehougs plass.

For a lively street food, go to the **Vippa** by the waterfront at Aker-shusstranda 25. This market has food stalls with dishes from all over the world. *You should try the bao buns or tacos and finish your meal with a waffle for dessert.* Vippa is open from noon to late evening and is a great place to grab a quick bite and enjoy the bustling atmosphere. You can get there by taking tram line 12 to Rådhusplassen and walking for about 10 minutes, or by bus lines 32 or 54 to Vippetangen.

In August, the **Oslo Food Festival** at Youngstorget. This event celebrates local food producers and has food stalls, cooking classes, and tasting sessions. *It's a fantastic way to explore the local food scene and try unique dishes.* Entry is usually free, but bring some cash for the food and drinks. You can reach Youngstorget by taking tram lines 11, 17, or 18 to Brugata, or by bus lines 34, 37, or 54 to Hammersborggata.

SHOPPING AND NIGHTLIFE

For some shopping, head straight to Karl Johans gate. This main street is a shopper's paradise, filled with everything from high-end designer shops to unique boutiques and popular chain stores. As you walk along, you'll find **Steen & Strøm**, a luxurious department store where you can browse through high-end fashion, beauty products, and home goods, showcasing both local designers and international brands. Located at Nedre Slottsgate 8, you can reach it easily by taking the tram to Stortinget or the metro to Jernbanetorget. Prices vary, but expect to pay premium prices for top-quality goods. Look out for Norwegian brands like Holzweiler and Swims.

If you're looking for something more eclectic, **Grünerløkka** is the place to be. This trendy neighborhood is known for its vintage stores, quirky boutiques, and artisan shops. Wander through the streets to discover second-hand clothes, handmade jewelry, and local art. One must-visit spot is **Robot**, a store specializing in vinyl records, located at Thorvald Meyers gate 32. Another is **Frøken Dianas Salonger**, which offers a mix of vintage clothing and accessories at Markveien 33. Don't miss the Sunday market at Blå, located at Brenneriveien 9, where you can browse stalls filled with crafts, food, and unique antiques along the river. To get to Grünerløkka, take tram lines 11, 12, or 13 to Olaf Ryes Plass.

For local crafts and traditional souvenirs, **Aker Brygge and Tjuvholmen** are must-visits. These scenic waterfront areas not only offer beautiful views of the harbor but also house a variety of shops selling traditional knitwear, contemporary art, and unique gifts. Aker Brygge is located near the city center, and you can reach it by taking tram line 12 to Aker Brygge. Stroll along the promenade, enjoy the public art installations, and visit shops like **Oleana**, known for its high-quality knitwear, and **Galleri Fineart**, which showcases contemporary Norwegian art. Prices can range from affordable trinkets to high-end artworks.

When the sun sets as you know already, the city's nightlife comes alive, especially around **Youngstorget**. This lively square is surrounded by popular bars and clubs. Begin the evening at **Kulturhuset**, located at Youngs gate 6, a multi-level venue offering live music, DJs, and even ping pong tables. It's a great spot to grab a drink and relax with friends before heading to nearby clubs like **The Villa**, known for its electronic music scene and located at Møllergata 23. Entry fees for clubs typically range from 100 to 200 NOK. You can reach Youngstorget by taking tram lines 11, 17, or 18 to Brugata, or bus lines 34, 37, or 54 to Hammersborggata.

Aker Brygge also transforms into a lively hub in the evening. Try a drink at one of the many bars along the waterfront, like **Ling Ling by Hakkasan**, which offers creative cocktails and breathtaking views. Ling Ling is located at Stranden 30 and can be reached by tram line 12 to Aker Brygge. For a more relaxed vibe, visit **Himkok**, a speakeasy-style bar at Storgata 27, famous for its innovative craft cocktails and cozy atmosphere. Himkok is a hidden gem but well worth the effort. Expect to pay around 120-150 NOK for a cocktail.

For some cultural spots, consider spending the evening at the **Oslo Opera House**.

Where is located at Kirsten Flagstads Plass 1, near the central station, you can catch an opera or ballet performance and admire the stunning architecture and panoramic views from the rooftop. Tickets for performances vary but typically start at around 300 NOK. For a different cultural outing, head to **Parkteatret** in Grünerløkka. This historic cinema at Olaf Ryes Plass has been transformed into a concert venue that hosts a variety of live music performances and events. Ticket prices for events vary, usually ranging from 200 to 400 NOK.

Safety at night here is generally good, but stay aware of your surroundings and stick to well-lit areas, especially when walking alone. Public transportation is reliable and safe for getting around after dark. Trams, buses, and the metro run frequently until late, and there are night buses that operate after regular hours. Taxis are also safe and can be easily found or booked via apps like Oslo Taxi or Uber.

During the winter months, the Christmas markets at Spikersuppa, located near Karl Johans gate. These markets feature festive stalls selling crafts, gifts, and delicious food and drinks, creating a magical atmosphere in the heart of the city. It's a perfect place to get into the holiday spirit, enjoy some warm treats, and find beautiful Christmas gifts.

NAVIGATING THE CITY

To visit this city, start with key landmarks like the Royal Palace and Akershus Fortress. The Royal Palace, at the end of Karl Johans gate, opens for guided tours in summer, costing about 135 NOK for adults and 100 NOK for students and seniors. It's easy to reach by taking the tram to Nationaltheatret or Stortinget. The palace grounds are always open and free to explore, perfect for a relaxed stroll. **Akershus Fortress offers a blend of history and scenic views.** Near the harbor, it's open daily from 6 AM to 9 PM with free entry to the grounds, and there's a museum inside with a small fee of around 100 NOK for adults. You can get there by taking tram lines 12 or 13 to Kontraskjæret or walking from the city center.

Use the city's extensive public transportation network for convenience. The network of trams, buses, and the metro, called the T-bane, makes getting around easy. Tickets are available at stations or via the Ruter app. A single ticket is valid for an hour on all transport modes. For more flexibility, get a 24-hour or 7-day pass.

Grünerløkka is the go-to area for quirky shopping and local culture. This nice neighborhood is known for quirky boutiques, vintage stores, and artisan shops. Visit Robot at Thorvald Meyers gate 32 for vinyl records or Frøken Dianas Salonger at Markveien 33 for vintage clothing and accessories. The Sunday market at Blå on Brenneriveien 9 offers crafts, food, and antiques. Reach Grünerløkka by taking tram lines 11, 12, or 13 to Olaf Ryes Plass. *Exploring these shops gives you a unique taste of the local scene.*

Vigeland Park is a must-see for art lovers. Located in Frogner, it's famous for over 200 sculptures by Gustav Vigeland. Open 24/7 and free to enter, it's a beautiful place for a stroll or picnic. Take tram lines 12 or 15 to Vigelandsparken and enjoy the impressive artworks and lush gardens.

The Oslo Opera House as i told you before is a modern architectural. Near the central station at Kirsten Flagstads Plass 1, it's an architectural marvel where you can walk on the roof for panoramic views. The building is open from 10 AM to 6 PM, and performance tickets start around 300 NOK. Nearby, the Munch Museum at Edvard Munchs Plass 1 showcases works by the famous painter, including "The Scream." Open daily from 10 AM to 6 PM, tickets cost about 160 NOK for adults. Take the metro to Tøyen or the bus to Munchmuseet to get there. *Walking on the Opera House roof offers stunning views.*

The Bygdøy Peninsula is rich with museums. The Fram Museum at Bygdøynesveien 39 showcases the polar ship Fram. Open daily from 10 AM to 5 PM, tickets are 120 NOK for adults. The nearby Viking Ship Museum at Huk Aveny 35 displays well-preserved Viking ships and artifacts. It's open from 9 AM to 6 PM in the summer and 10 AM to 4 PM in the winter, with an admission fee of 120 NOK for adults. Reach these museums by taking bus number 30 to Bygdøynes.

Learn about peace and history at the Nobel Peace Center. Located at Brynjulf Bulls Plass 1 near City Hall, it offers exhibitions on the Nobel Peace Prize and its laureates. Open from 10 AM to 6 PM, tickets are about 140 NOK for adults. Get there by taking tram line 12 to Aker Brygge or bus lines 31, 32, or 54. *The exhibitions here are both educational and inspiring.*

3 BERGEN

Bergen, known as the gateway to the fjords, is a city with a nice history. With about 280,000 people and covering 465 square kilometers, it's the second-largest city in the country. Nestled between seven mountains and the sea, this coastal city is famous for its stunning landscapes and vibrant culture.

Is located on the west coast, this city is the best start visiting the fjords. One of the main attractions you must see is **Bryggen Wharf**, a UNESCO World Heritage site with colorful wooden houses from the Hanseatic League era. Walking through Bryggen, you feel the history in the narrow alleys and quaint shops.

Take the **Fløibanen Funicular** up to **Mount Fløyen** for breathtaking views over the city and fjords. This spot is great for hiking, with trails for all levels. The funicular runs daily, and tickets are affordable.

Visit the **Hanseatic Museum** in one of the old wooden houses on Bryggen to learn about the life of the Hanseatic merchants. Also, see the **Bergenhus Fortress**, one of the oldest and best-preserved fortresses in the country, which played a key role in the city's defense.

If you love seafood, go to the **Fish Market** for fresh salmon, king crab, and shrimp. It's a lively place to enjoy a meal and soak in the local atmosphere.

The city is also known for the **Bergen International Festival**, featuring music, dance, and theater performances from around the world. Held in late May and early June, it is one of the most important cultural events in the region.

Historically, this city has been a vital trading hub. Its strategic location made it a key player in the Hanseatic League, an important medieval trade alliance. Over the centuries, the city has grown and evolved but still keeps much of its historical charm. The mix of medieval architecture and modern life makes it a special place to visit for sure!

ATTRACTIONS

Bryggen Wharf is a historical gem dating back to the 14th century.

The colorful wooden houses here were once bustling with German merchants. Now, they are filled with narrow alleyways and charming shops that transport you back in time. The best time to visit Bryggen is in the morning when it's less crowded. Most shops and museums open around 10 AM. Walking around is free, but visiting attractions like the **Hanseatic Museum** costs about 100 NOK. This museum is in one of the old wooden houses and offers guided tours that provide deep insights into the lives of the merchants who worked here. You can get here easily by walking from the city center or taking tram line 1 to the Byparken stop.

Right next to Bryggen, you'll find the **Hanseatic Museum**, which dives deep into the lives of the merchants. The museum opens daily from 10 AM to 5 PM, and admission is around 120 NOK for adults. St. Mary's Church, the city's oldest building, dates back to the 12th century and has impressive Romanesque architecture. It's open from 11 AM to 3 PM daily, with an entrance fee of 50 NOK.

For a delicious meal, try **Bryggeloftet & Stuene**, which offers traditional dishes like fish soup and reindeer steak, with main courses ranging from 200 to 400 NOK. For fine dining, **To Kokker** is known for its exquisite seafood, where a three-course meal costs about 600 NOK. For something casual, **Baker Brun** is perfect for coffee and pastries, with prices around 50 NOK for a pastry and coffee. Staying near Bryggen is convenient; the **Radisson Blu Royal Hotel** costs about 1500 NOK per night and offers luxurious accommodations with stunning views of the harbor. The **Clarion Hotel Admiral**, with rates around 1300 NOK per night, is another excellent choice within walking distance.

The **Fish Market** at Torget is another must-see. Operating since the 1200s, it's a lively hub where you can immerse yourself in the local food culture. The market is open daily from early morning until late afternoon, but the best time to visit is early, around 8-9 AM, to catch the freshest seafood. Here, you can taste local dishes directly from the stalls, with some vendors cooking meals on the spot. Fresh seafood like salmon, king crab, and shrimp are available, with prices varying depending on the catch but typically around 200 NOK for a meal. The Fish Market is easily accessible by tram line 1 or bus number 3 to the Torget stop.

Near the Fish Market, you have a variety of dining options. **Fisketorget** and **Enhjørningen** are top choices for fresh seafood, offering dishes like grilled salmon and seafood platters, with main courses costing between 250 to 400 NOK. **Bare Vestland** is great for traditional dishes with a modern twist, where you can try their set menu for about 450 NOK. For an upscale dining experience, **Cornelius Seafood Restaurant**, accessible by a short boat ride, offers gourmet seafood meals with prices starting at 700 NOK for a three-course dinner. If you need a place to stay, the **Thon Hotel Rosenkrantz** is nearby and offers comfortable accommodations for around 1200 NOK per night, including breakfast. Another great option is the **Magic Hotel Korskirken**, known for its modern design and central location, with rates around 1000 NOK per night.

Fløyen Mountain provides breathtaking panoramic views of the city and surrounding fjords. To get there, you can take the Fløibanen Funicular, which runs daily from early morning until late evening. Round trip tickets cost about 95 NOK for adults and 50 NOK for children. Visiting early in the morning or late in the afternoon is ideal to avoid crowds and enjoy the serene beauty of the sunrise or sunset. At the top, you'll find several hiking trails suitable for all levels, a café, and a souvenir shop. You can reach the Fløibanen station by walking from the city center or taking tram line 1 to the Fløibanen stop.

At the summit, you can visit beyond the hiking trails. There's a troll forest and playground, making it a fun destination for families. Renting bikes to explore scenic routes is another great suggestion. Dining at the **Fløien Folkerestaurant** provides a cozy setting with spectacular views, where main courses cost around 200-300 NOK. For something casual, the **Brushytten Café** offers snacks and beverages with prices around 50-100 NOK. If you plan to stay nearby, the **Clarion Hotel Admiral** is a short walk from the funicular station, offering rooms for around 1300 NOK per night. Another excellent choice is the **Hotel Norge by Scandic**, offering luxury and comfort with easy access to both the city center and Fløibanen, with rates starting at 1500 NOK per night.

Visiting the city using public transportation is efficient and straightforward. The tram system covers most areas, with tram line 1 being particularly useful as it connects many main attractions. Buses are also reliable, with routes 3 and 5 providing frequent service to key spots. As you may know already, utilizing apps like Google Maps and the Ruter app will help you find the best routes and schedules. So, why not using it. For real-time updates and easier navigation, Citymapper is highly recommended.

For assistance and more information, visit the **Oslo Visitor Centre** at Østbanehallen near the central station. They offer maps, brochures, and advice on what to see and do, and can help with booking tours and tickets.Walking is also a great option, as many attractions are close to each other. Just wear comfortable shoes and visit. Ferries provide a scenic way to travel. From the pier near City Hall, you can take a ferry to the Bygdøy Peninsula to visit the Viking Ship Museum and Fram Museum. Ferries are included in the public transport ticket, making it affordable to visit fjord.

LOCAL CUISINE

For the best seafood and regional specialties, you should start at **Enhjørningen**, which is in one of the historic wooden buildings at Bryggen Wharf. They are famous for their seafood dishes, especially the fish soup and halibut. It's best to visit early in the evening around 6 PM to avoid the dinner rush. You can easily reach it by taking tram line 1 to the Byparken stop and then walking a short distance to Bryggen.

Another fantastic spot is **Fisketorget**, right at the Fish Market on Torget. Here, you can enjoy fresh catches like salmon, king crab, and shrimp. The market is open daily from early morning until late afternoon, but for the freshest selection, go early around 8-9 AM. The market stalls also serve ready-to-eat meals like fish cakes and seafood platters. It's accessible by tram line 1 or bus number 3 to the Torget stop.

For a fine dining experience, head to **Cornelius Seafood Restaurant**, located on a nearby island. You'll need to take a boat ride from the pier near Bryggen, which adds to the experience. They serve gourmet seafood dishes, with a three-course dinner starting at about 700 NOK. The boat ride provides scenic views of the fjord. The restaurant is very popular, so make sure to book in advance and aim for a late afternoon reservation to enjoy the sunset during your meal.

Bryggeloftet & Stuene, also at Bryggen, offers a cozy atmosphere with traditional dishes like reindeer steak and fish soup. Main courses range from 200 to 400 NOK. It's a good idea to book a table for dinner around 5 PM to beat the crowds. You can get there by walking from the city center or taking tram line 1 to the Byparken stop.

For casual dining, **Pingvinen** at Vaskerelven 14 is a local favorite known for its hearty Norwegian comfort food. Try the lamb stew or the fish cakes. Prices are reasonable, with main courses around 150-250 NOK. The restaurant is usually busy, so visiting for an early lunch around 11 AM is a good idea. It's easily reachable by tram line 1 to Byparken, followed by a short walk.

If you're looking for street food, visit the **Street Food Bergen** market at Kong Oscars gate 10. Open from 11 AM to 8 PM, this market offers a variety of street food from different cultures, including local specialties. It's an excellent place to grab a quick and tasty bite. You can reach it by taking tram line 1 to Byparken and then walking for about 10 minutes.

If you are vegetarian or vegan, **Pygmalion Økocafe & Galleri** at Nedre Korskirkeallmenningen 4 is a great location. They offer a variety of vegetarian dishes, like their famous vegan burger. Main courses cost around 150-200 NOK. It's best to visit around 2 PM for a late lunch to avoid the busiest hours. The café is a short walk from the city center and easily accessible by tram line 1 to Byparken.

Another excellent option is **Daily Pot** at Vestre Torggaten 9, which serves healthy bowls and soups with plenty of vegetarian and vegan choices. Prices range from 100 to 150 NOK for a meal. Visit around 1 PM for lunch. It's located near the main shopping area and is reachable by tram line 1 to Byparken, followed by a short walk.

For food festivals, check out the **Bergen Matfestival** held in late August at Bryggen. This festival celebrates local food producers and offers a chance to taste a wide range of local dishes. Entry is free, but bring some cash for food and drinks. The festival is easy to reach by walking from the city center or taking tram line 1 to Byparken.

FESTIVALS AND EVENTS

The **Bergen International Festival** is a cornerstone of the city's cultural scene, running from late May to early June. Established in 1953, it is the largest festival in the Nordic countries, offering a wide range of events that include music, dance, theater, and visual arts. The festival is known for its high-quality performances and international artists. Venues like Grieg Hall, the National Stage, and various outdoor locations host the events. **Key activities** include classical concerts, contemporary dance performances, theater shows, and art exhibitions. For a unique experience, attend the opening ceremony at Torgallmenningen Square. Tickets range from 200 to 600 NOK, depending on the event. You may need to **Book early** to secure your spot. Most venues are close to the city center, easily reachable by tram line 1 to Byparken.

During the festival, stay at **Radisson Blu Royal Hotel** at Bryggen, which offers rooms from 1500 NOK per night, a restaurant, fitness center, and free Wi-Fi. Alternatively, the **Clarion Hotel Admiral** at C. Sundts gate 9 provides waterfront views, a restaurant, and breakfast included, with rooms starting around 1300 NOK per night.

Bergenfest, held in mid-June at the historic Bergenhus Fortress, focuses on contemporary music. Established in 1993, the festival features a diverse lineup of international and local artists across rock, pop, and indie genres. The fortress, one of the best-preserved in Norway, provides a stunning backdrop. **Key activities** include main stage performances, intimate acoustic sets, and food stalls offering local delicacies. Tickets range from 800 to 1500 NOK for the full festival, with day passes also available. **Dress comfortably** for outdoor weather and prepare for a mix of rain and sunshine. The fortress is within walking distance from the city center or reachable by tram line 1 to Bryggen.

For Bergenfest, consider staying at **Magic Hotel Korskirken** at Nedre Korskirkeallmenningen 1, offering modern rooms from 1200 NOK per night, a rooftop terrace, and free Wi-Fi. **Thon Hotel Rosenkrantz** at Rosenkrantz-gaten 7 has rooms from 1400 NOK per night, including breakfast and evening meals.

The **Bergen Food Festival** in late August at Bryggen celebrates local food producers and culinary traditions. The festival features cooking demonstrations, food tastings, and stalls selling fresh produce and regional specialties. **Key activities** include live cooking shows by top chefs, workshops on traditional food preparation, and plenty of opportunities to sample local dishes like fish cakes, reindeer sausages, and sweet Norwegian pastries. **Entry is free**, but bring cash for food purchases. The best time to visit is in the morning to avoid the crowds. You can reach Bryggen by walking from the city center or taking tram line 1 to Byparken.

Stay at the **Clarion Hotel Admiral**, close to Bryggen, during the food festival. The hotel includes breakfast and offers rooms from 1300 NOK per night. Start your day with breakfast at the hotel, then explore the festival for lunch and dinner.

Nattjazz Festival, held at the end of May at USF Verftet, is one of Europe's longest-running jazz festivals, established in 1972. This festival spans about ten days and features a mix of international and local jazz artists. The venue, USF Verftet, is an old sardine factory turned cultural center, providing a unique setting for the concerts. **Key activities** include nightly jazz performances, jam sessions, and workshops. Tickets range from 350 to 500 NOK per night, with a festival pass available for jazz enthusiasts. To reach USF Verftet, take bus number 11 from the city center to Verftet.

For Nattjazz, stay at **Hotel Norge by Scandic** at Nedre Ole Bulls Plass 4, offering modern amenities and rooms from 1600 NOK per night, with a gym, spa, and breakfast included. **Pygmalion Økocafe & Galleri** at Nedre

Korskirkeallmenningen 4 serves organic vegetarian and vegan dishes, perfect for a pre-concert meal.

The **Bergen International Film Festival (BIFF)**, established in 2000, is held in late September and showcases films from around the world, including documentaries, feature films, and shorts. Screenings take place at venues like Bergen Kino and the University of Bergen. **Key activities** include film premieres, director Q&A sessions, and panel discussions on various film topics. Tickets cost around 100 NOK per screening, with festival passes available. Dress comfortably for long film-watching days and plan your schedule to catch your must-see films. Venues are easily accessible by tram line 1 to Byparken.

During BIFF, stay at **Magic Hotel Korskirken** for proximity to screenings, with rooms from 1200 NOK per night and modern amenities. For dining, try **Daily Pot** at Vestre Torggaten 9 for healthy bowls and soups or **Baker Brun** for quick bites between films.

VISIT THE CITY

You can start with **Bryggen Wharf**, the historic harbor district with colorful wooden houses from the Hanseatic era. This UNESCO World Heritage site shows the city's rich past. Walking around is free, but for deeper insights, join a guided tour. Bryggen is located centrally, easily reachable by walking from the city center or taking tram line 1 to the Byparken stop. Most shops and museums at Bryggen open around 10 AM. Wander through the narrow alleys, visit small shops, and stop by the **Hanseatic Museum** to learn about the merchants' lives. The museum charges around 120 NOK for entry and is open from 10 AM to 5 PM.

Next, head to the **Fløibanen Funicular** for stunning views of the city and fjords from Mount Fløyen.

Eivor Eriksen

The funicular operates daily from early morning until late evening, with round-trip tickets costing about 95 NOK for adults and 50 NOK for children. The Fløibanen station is located at Vetrlidsallmenningen 21, a short walk from the city center, or you can take tram line 1 to the Fløibanen stop. Once at the top, explore several hiking trails, enjoy a meal at the café, and pick up a souvenir from the shop. There's also a playground for children and a troll forest, making it a great family outing.

Don't miss the **Fish Market** at Torget, operational since the 1200s. Arrive early, around 8-9 AM, to see the freshest catches of the day. Open daily from 7 AM to 7 PM, the market offers local seafood like salmon and king crab. Try the fish cakes and seafood platters from various stalls. The market is easily accessible by tram line 1 or bus number 3 to the Torget stop. It's a lively spot to grab a quick, delicious meal or to pick up fresh ingredients for cooking.

For a bit of history, visit **Bergenhus Fortress**, one of the oldest fortifications in Norway, located near the harbor. Open daily from 6 AM to 9 PM, the grounds are free to explore. Inside, you'll find the **Håkon's Hall** and **Rosenkrantz Tower**, which offer deeper insights into the medieval history of the fortress. Tickets for the hall and tower are about 100 NOK each. Walk through the medieval halls and towers, and enjoy the surrounding park. It's a short walk from the city center or reachable by tram line 1 to Bryggen.

If you love art, the **KODE Art Museums and Composer Homes** are essential. Located at Rasmus Meyers allé 3, KODE consists of several buildings showcasing art from various periods, including works by Edvard Munch. The museums are open from 11 AM to 5 PM, Tuesday through Sunday, and a combined ticket costs around 150 NOK for adults. Reach KODE by walking from the city center or taking tram line 1 to the Byparken stop. Don't miss the chance to visit the composer homes of Edvard Grieg, Harald Sæverud, and Ole Bull, located in scenic surroundings outside the city center, often accessible by a short bus or taxi ride.

For a unique historical experience, visit the **Leprosy Museum** at St. Jørgen's Hospital, which offers insights into the history of leprosy treatment. The museum is open from 11 AM to 3 PM, with an entrance fee of around 80 NOK. Located at Kong Oscars gate 59, it's reachable by bus number 11 from the city center. The museum provides a poignant look at how patients lived and were treated, offering guided tours that enrich the visit.

Another key attraction is the **Aquarium**, situated at Nordnesbakken 4, showcasing a variety of marine life, including seals, penguins, and fish from around the world. The aquarium is open daily from 10 AM to 6 PM, with tickets costing about 300 NOK for adults and 200 NOK for children. To get there, take bus number 11 to Nordnes. Inside, you can watch feeding shows, participate in educational talks, and enjoy interactive exhibits.

The tram, especially line 1, covers most key areas, including the city center, Bryggen, and major attractions. Buses are also reliable, with routes like number 3 and 5 providing frequent service to important spots. For day trips, consider getting a Bergen Card, which offers unlimited travel on public transport and discounts on attractions.

Walking is another great option since many attractions are close to each other. For longer distances, consider renting a bike; several rental stations are scattered around the city.

Prices are generally affordable, with hourly rates or daily passes available. You can rent a bike for around 100 NOK per day, giving you the freedom to visit as you want. Some popular bike rental services include **Bergen Bysykkel** and **Rent-A-Bike Bergen**, both offering well-maintained bicycles suitable for city exploration. Many are located near major attractions and public transport hubs, such as Bryggen, the Fish Market, and the train station, making it easy to switch between walking, biking, and public transport as needed.

4 THE FJORDS

The fjords of Norway have deep blue waters and towering cliffs. These amazing formations were created during the Ice Age when glaciers carved out deep valleys, which later filled with seawater. One of the most famous is the **Sognefjord**, known as the "King of the Fjords." It stretches over 200 kilometers inland and reaches depths of up to 1,308 meters. You can easily get here from Bergen, which is a common starting point for tours.

In Sognefjord, you should visit the village of Flåm. The **Flåm Railway**

is one of the steepest and most scenic train rides in the world, offering stunning views of waterfalls and steep mountainsides. A round trip ticket costs about 550 NOK, and the train runs multiple times a day. You can also enjoy kayaking on the calm waters, surrounded by high cliffs, or take a boat tour to get closer to the landscape. Hiking is another great option, with trails offering amazing views.

Geirangerfjord is another must-see. This fjord is known for its dramatic scenery, with steep cliffs and beautiful waterfalls like the Seven Sisters and the Suitor. It is about 15 kilometers long and 260 meters deep. You can access it from the town of Ålesund. Drive up to the **Dalsnibba viewpoint** for panoramic views of the fjord. Entry costs 150 NOK per vehicle. The village of Geiranger is charming, with a small museum and plenty of local history. Cruises are popular here too, costing around 300 NOK for a 90-minute tour.

Here are many activities that you can enjoy. Fishing is great, with many spots to catch local fish. Hiking trails range from easy to challenging, all offering incredible views. Wildlife watching is also a treat – you might see seals, porpoises, and various birds. So i am recommend to try.

GEIRANGERFJORD AND NÆRØYFJORD

Geirangerfjord is one of the most stunning natural wonders you'll ever see for sure! For the best views, go to the **Dalsnibba viewpoint**, about 20 kilometers from Geiranger village. This spot will give you a breathtaking look at the fjord, with snow-capped mountains and deep blue waters. Drive up to Dalsnibba on the Nibbevegen toll road, which costs 150 NOK per vehicle. The viewpoint is open from late May to early October, depending on the weather. It's best to visit early in the morning or late in the afternoon to avoid crowds and get the best light for photos.

For hiking, the **Storseterfossen Trail** is a great choice. The trail starts near Westerås Farm, just a short drive from Geiranger village. The hike takes about 2 hours round trip and leads you to the Storseterfossen waterfall, where you can walk behind the falls. The trail is well-marked and moderately easy. Another hike to try is the **Flydalsjuvet viewpoint**, located about 4 kilometers from Geiranger. This short walk from the parking area offers nice views of the fjord and is perfect for photos.

Visiting Geirangerfjord by boat is a must. You can take a **fjord cruise** from Geiranger harbor. These cruises last about 90 minutes and cost around 300 NOK. You'll get fantastic views of waterfalls like the Seven Sisters and the Suitor. If you want more adventure, rent a kayak and paddle close to the waterfalls and cliffs. Kayak rentals start at about 200 NOK per hour, and guided tours are available for a safer and more informative experience.

Getting to Geirangerfjord is easy. If you're driving, it takes about 2.5 hours from Ålesund. Public buses are available but less frequent, so check schedules in advance. For accommodations, stay at the **Hotel Union** in Geiranger, located at Geirangervegen 100. Rooms start from 1,800 NOK per night and include amenities like a spa, indoor pool, and stunning fjord views.

For dining, you can try the **Brasserie Posten** at Geirangervegen 4, which serves local Norwegian cuisine with a modern twist. It's open daily from 11 AM to 10 PM. Another option is the **Westerås Farm**, where you can enjoy traditional dishes in a cozy setting, surrounded by beautiful scenery. It's open from 12 PM to 8 PM and also offers a café with lighter options.

Nærøyfjord is another good spot. For the best views, visit the **Stegastein viewpoint**, a platform extending 30 meters out from the mountainside and 650 meters above the fjord. Stegastein is about a 15-minute drive from Flåm along the Aurlandsvegen road. There is no entry fee, and the viewpoint is open year-round, though the road may close in winter due to snow.

For hiking, try the **Nærøyfjord Trail** from Gudvangen to Bakka. This trail is about 6 kilometers long and relatively easy, taking you through beautiful landscapes along the water. Another popular hike is up to the **Rimstigen** viewpoint, which starts in the village of Bakka. This challenging trail takes about 3 hours to climb but rewards you with incredible views of the fjord below.

Boat tours are a great way to visit Nærøyfjord. You can take a **sightseeing ferry** from Flåm to Gudvangen, costing about 400 NOK and taking around two hours. These tours provide stunning views of steep cliffs and waterfalls. For a more active experience, rent a kayak in Flåm or Gudvangen, with prices starting around 250 NOK per hour. Guided kayak tours are also available, offering safety equipment and expert insights.

To get to Nærøyfjord, drive from Bergen, which takes about 2 hours along the scenic E16 road. Trains to Flåm are another option, offering beautiful views along the way. In Flåm, stay at the **Fretheim Hotel**, located at Flåms-brygga 1. Rooms start around 1,500 NOK per night, offering fantastic views and easy access to the fjord.

For dining in Flåm, visit the **Ægir BrewPub**, located at Flåmsbrygga. It's open daily from 12 PM to 11 PM and offers a variety of local dishes and craft beers brewed on-site. Another great spot is the **Flåmstova Restaurant**, which serves traditional Norwegian food and is open from 11 AM to 10 PM.

The best time to visit is during the summer months, from June to August, when the weather is mild and the days are long. Guided tours are available for both Geirangerfjord and Nærøyfjord, offering boat trips, hikes, and even cycling tours. These tours provide expert knowledge and often include transportation and meals, making your visit hassle-free.

HIKING AND OUTDOOR ACTIVITIES

Storseterfossen Trail You start your hike at **Westerås Farm**, located at Vesterås, 6216 Geiranger. This 5-kilometer round trip trail leads you through lush landscapes and ends at the Storseterfossen waterfall, where you can walk behind the falls. The hike takes about 2 hours and is moderately easy. It's best from May to October. Westerås Farm also offers a restaurant and accommodations, making it a great rest stop. There's no entry fee, and parking is available at the farm.

For beautiful views, head to **Flydalsjuvet Viewpoint**, 4 kilometers from Geiranger at Flydalsjuvet, 6216 Geiranger. The trail is an easy 30-minute walk from the parking area and offers stunning views, especially in summer. This viewpoint is open year-round, with no entry fee and free parking.

Skageflå Farm For a more challenging hike, visit **Skageflå Farm**. Take a boat from Geiranger harbor to the trailhead, costing about 300 NOK. The hike is steep, about 2.5 kilometers one way, and takes around 2 hours. Best hiked from May to September, the farm offers panoramic views of the fjord and a glimpse into traditional Norwegian life. Boats depart multiple times daily.

Kayaking in Geirangerfjord Rent kayaks from **Geiranger Kayak Center** at Homlong, close to the village center. Prices start at 200 NOK per hour. Guided tours are about 600 NOK for a half-day trip, including equipment and historical insights. The best time for kayaking is June to August when the waters are calm and warm.

RIB Boat Safari For an exhilarating experience, take a RIB boat safari. These high-speed boats take you close to the cliffs and waterfalls. Tours last about 1.5 hours and cost around 700 NOK. They depart from Geiranger harbor daily from May to September.

Wildlife Watching is another must. Early mornings or late afternoons are best for spotting seals, porpoises, and various bird species. A wildlife safari tour costs about 500 NOK per person and includes expert guides. These tours leave from Geiranger harbor and last about 2 hours.

Where to Stay and Eat in Geiranger

Stay at **Hotel Union**, located at Geirangervegen 100. Rooms start at 1,800 NOK per night. The hotel is open year-round and features a spa, indoor pool, and stunning views. It's the perfect place to relax after a day of exploring.

For dining, try **Brasserie Posten** at Geirangervegen 4. Open daily from 11 AM to 10 PM, it serves local Norwegian cuisine with a modern twist. The restaurant is known for its fresh ingredients and innovative dishes.

Another great option is **Westerås Farm**, open from 12 PM to 8 PM. It serves traditional dishes in a cozy setting surrounded by beautiful scenery. The farm also features a café for lighter options and is located at Vesterås, 6216 Geiranger.

Hiking Trails and Outdoor Activities in Nærøyfjord

The **Nærøyfjord Trail** from Gudvangen to Bakka is a must-do. This 6-kilometer trail is an easy, scenic walk that takes around 2 hours. Best hiked from June to September, the trail offers nice views and doesn't require permits. It starts in Gudvangen, accessible by road.

For a more challenging hike, as i told you before the **Rimstigen Trail** starts in Bakka and climbs steeply for 2 kilometers. It takes about 3 hours to reach the top, with incredible panoramic views. Best from June to September, the trailhead is in Bakka, easily accessible by road.

Kayaking in Nærøyfjord, Rent kayaks in Flåm or Gudvangen. Prices start around 250 NOK per hour. Guided tours provide safety equipment and insights. Paddle through the fjord, getting close to cliffs and waterfalls. Rentals are available at **Njord Kayak Center** in Flåm, located at Flåmsbrygga 1.

Boat Tours, Taking a boat tour is a great way to explore Nærøyfjord. The ferry from Flåm to Gudvangen costs about 400 NOK and takes around two hours. These tours offer stunning views of the cliffs and waterfalls and run frequently during the summer. Depart from Flåm harbor at Flåmsbrygga.

For the best views, visit the **Stegastein Viewpoint**. This platform extends 30 meters from the mountainside and is 650 meters above the fjord. It's a 15-minute drive from Flåm on the Aurlandsvegen road. The viewpoint is open year-round, though the road may close in winter. There's no entry fee, and you can drive or join a guided tour.

Where to Stay and Eat in Nærøyfjord

In Flåm, stay at the **Fretheim Hotel**, located at Flåmsbrygga 1. Rooms start around 1,500 NOK per night. The hotel is historic with modern amenities and offers fantastic views. It's open year-round and is a perfect base for exploring the area.

Ægir BrewPub, For dining, visit the **Ægir BrewPub** at Flåmsbrygga. Open daily from 12 PM to 11 PM, it serves local dishes and craft beers brewed on-site. The pub has a cozy, Viking-inspired atmosphere and is a great place to relax.

Another great dining spot is the **Flåmstova Restaurant**, serving traditional Norwegian food. Open from 11 AM to 10 PM, the restaurant's cozy atmosphere and delicious meals make it a favorite among visitors. It's located at Flåmsbrygga 1, right in the heart of Flåm.

The best time to visit these areas is during the summer months, from June to August, when the weather is mild, and the days are long. Guided tours are available for both Geirangerfjord and Nærøyfjord, offering boat trips, hikes, and even cycling tours.

FJORDS BY BOAT

GEIRANGERFJORD BOAT TOURS

Geiranger Fjordservice AS offers the **Geirangerfjord Cruise** which lasts about 1.5 hours and costs around 300 NOK. The tours run from May to September, with frequent departures throughout the day. You can reach Geiranger by car via Route 63 or by bus from Ålesund, which is about a 2.5-hour drive. On this tour, expect to see famous waterfalls like the Seven Sisters and the Suitor up close. The boats are equipped with comfortable seating, big windows, and outdoor decks. You'll also get interesting facts about the fjord's history and geology.

Another great option located at Geiranger harbor is **Norway Fjord Travel**. They offer the **Classic Geirangerfjord Sightseeing Tour**. This tour also lasts about 1.5 hours and costs approximately 350 NOK. Running from May to October with multiple daily departures, the tour features both indoor and outdoor seating, and detailed commentary on the area. To reach Geiranger, you can drive or take a bus from nearby cities like Ålesund or Oslo.

RIB Adventures Geiranger For a thrilling ride, check out **RIB Adventures Geiranger**. Their **RIB Boat Safari** costs around 700 NOK and lasts for 1 hour. Tours run daily from May to September, departing from Geiranger harbor. You can reach Geiranger by car or bus. These high-speed boats take you close to the cliffs and waterfalls at exhilarating speeds, and the guides share fascinating stories about the area.

NÆRØYFJORD BOAT TOURS

FjordSafari Norway offers the **Nærøyfjord Safari**. This intimate 2-hour tour costs around 600 NOK. Smaller boats provide a more personal experience, and there's a good chance of spotting wildlife like seals and porpoises. Tours run from June to September with several departures throughout the day. You can reach Flåm by train from Bergen or Oslo, or by car via the E16 road. The guides provide engaging and informative commentary, ensuring you don't miss any details.

Norway in a Nutshell departs from both Bergen and Oslo and includes a scenic train ride along with a fjord cruise. The full-day tour costs about 1,500 NOK and runs year-round. The fjord cruise portion lasts about 2 hours, offering spectacular views and detailed commentary. To join this tour, take the train from either city to Flåm. This package makes it easy to experience multiple aspects of Norway's natural beauty.

Viking Cruises offers the **Ultimate Fjord Cruise** departing from Flåm harbor. This premium 3-hour tour costs approximately 1,200 NOK and includes a gourmet meal. Running from June to August, the cruise features luxury seating, large windows, and spacious outdoor decks. The leisurely pace allows for a deeper exploration, combining fine dining with stunning views. Flåm can be reached by train from Bergen or Oslo, or by car via the E16.

5 THE LOFOTEN ISLANDS

The **Lofoten Islands** are amazing. They have steep mountains, beautiful beaches, and charming fishing villages. These islands are part of Norway and are inside the Arctic Circle. They cover about 1,227 square kilometers and around 24,000 people live there.

To get to the Islands, you can drive on the E10 highway or take a ferry from Bodø. The islands stretch from near Narvik out into the Norwegian Sea. You'll see islands connected by bridges and tunnels.

You should definitely go to **Reine**. It's one of the most beautiful villages in the world.

You can hike **Reinebringen** here. This hike is about 2 kilometers round trip and takes around 2 hours. At the top, you get an incredible view of the mountains and fjords.

Nusfjord is another place you must see. It's one of Norway's oldest fishing villages. Walking through Nusfjord, you'll see traditional fishermen's cabins and old buildings. There's also a small museum where you can learn about the history of fishing in the area.

For Viking history, go to the **Lofotr Viking Museum** in Borg. This museum is built on the site of the largest Viking longhouse ever found. You'll see reconstructed buildings and artifacts. You can even join in Viking games and enjoy a Viking feast.

The islands are also known for the **Northern Lights**, which you can see from September to April. The skies are dark and there's little light pollution, making it perfect for watching this natural light show. In summer, from late May to mid-July, you can experience the **Midnight Sun**, where the sun doesn't set at all.

Fishing is a big part of life here. You can join a fishing trip to catch cod, halibut, and other fish. Local operators offer deep-sea fishing trips, which are a lot of fun and give you a taste of the local fishing tradition.

Kayaking is another great activity. You can rent a kayak or join a guided tour to explore the fjords and coastline up close. It's a peaceful way to see the islands, with the chance to spot wildlife and enjoy the scenery.

The Lofoten Islands have been inhabited for over a thousand years. Vikings lived here around 500 AD. This rich history is still alive in the culture and traditions you'll see today.

ATTRACTIONS

Kvalvika Beach is a secluded gem located on the northern coast of Moskenesøya. To get there, drive from Fredvang and park at the Torsfjord parking lot, which is accessible via the E10 highway. From the parking lot, the hike to the beach is about 2 kilometers and takes around an hour. The trail is moderately difficult, so wear good hiking shoes. There is no entry fee, and the beach is always open. Once there, you can enjoy the pristine sands, clear waters, and dramatic mountain scenery. Historically, this area was used by fishermen who set up seasonal camps to catch fish.

Henningsvær Village is located on several small islands off the southern coast of Austvågøya. Drive along the E10 and take the exit towards Henningsvær; it's a scenic route with beautiful coastal views. The village is known for its picturesque buildings and vibrant art scene. Visit the **Kaviar-Factory**, an art gallery housed in a former caviar factory, open daily from 11 AM to 5 PM, with an entry fee of 50 NOK. Walk through the narrow streets, explore local shops, and enjoy fresh seafood at one of the cozy cafes. The **Henningsvær Lighthouse** offers stunning sea views and is accessible by foot. The lighthouse is open to the public from 10 AM to 6 PM, and entry is free. Henningsvær has been a hub for fishing since the Viking Age, making it rich in maritime history.

The **Fishermen's Memorial** in Ballstad honors the fishermen who lost their lives at sea. Ballstad is a short drive from Leknes, following the E10 and then local roads to the village. The memorial is located in the heart of the village and is accessible at any time, free of charge. It's a somber but important part of the local heritage, with plaques listing the names of those who perished. Ballstad is one of the largest fishing villages in Lofoten, with a history dating back to the 19th century.

Unstad Beach is on the northern coast of Vestvågøya and is famous among surfers. Drive from Leknes via the E10 and follow signs to Unstad. The beach is open all year, and there's no entry fee. You can take surfing lessons from the Unstad Arctic Surf School, which operates daily from 9 AM to 6 PM, with lessons starting at 500 NOK. There's a small café at the beach offering hot drinks and local pastries, open from 10 AM to 5 PM. Historically, Unstad was a fishing village, but now it's known for its surfing culture.

For hiking, the **Mannen Hike** starts near Haukland Beach on Vestvågøya. Drive from Leknes via the E10 to Haukland, where you'll find parking. The hike is about 4 kilometers round trip and takes around 3 hours. The trail is moderately challenging, so wear sturdy hiking boots and bring water and snacks. The best time to hike is from May to September when the weather is mild. At the summit, you'll get panoramic views of the surrounding islands and sea. The trail is free to access and open at all times.

Eliassen Rorbuer in Hamnøy offers traditional fishermen's cabins with modern amenities. Located on the island of Moskenesøya, you can reach Hamnøy by driving along the E10. The cabins provide stunning views of the surrounding mountains and fjords. Prices start at 1,500 NOK per night. These rorbuer have been used by fishermen since the 19th century and have been updated to offer comfortable accommodations while retaining their historical charm.

STAYING IN RORBUER CABINS

These cabins are cozy, often with nice views of the fjords and mountains. Most of them have comfortable beds, a small kitchen, a living area, Wi-Fi, heating, and hot water.

Eliassen Rorbuer in Hamnøy is a top choice. Located on Moskenesøya, you can reach these cabins by driving along the E10 highway from either Moskenes or Å. When you arrive, you'll find breathtaking scenery all around. Prices start at around 1,500 NOK per night. Each cabin offers a tranquil retreat with beautiful views of the fjord and mountains. **Check-in is from 3 PM and check-out is by 11 AM.** Services include free parking, Wi-Fi, a restaurant on-site, and bike rentals.

Svinøya Rorbuer in Svolvær is another excellent option. Is located on a small island connected to Svolvær by a bridge, giving you easy access to the town's amenities while offering a secluded feel. Prices also start around 1,500 NOK per night. The cabins feature cozy wooden interiors and views of the harbor. To get there, drive along the E10 and follow the signs to Svolvær. **Check-in is from 2 PM and check-out is by 12 PM.** Services include a restaurant, Wi-Fi, guided tours, and fishing trips.

When booking, you may want to reserve your cabin several months in advance, especially during the busy summer season or holidays. Popular Websites like "Booking.com" and "Airbnb" list these cabins, but you can often find the best deals and availability by booking directly through the cabin's website.

If you're staying at **Eliassen Rorbuer**, you'll have easy access to several nearby attractions. Visit Reine and hike Reinebringen, a 2-kilometer round trip hike that takes about 2 hours and offers spectacular views. Explore the village of Å and visit the Norwegian Fishing Village Museum to learn about the area's rich fishing history. For dining, try **Anitas Sjømat** in Sakrisøy, known for its fresh seafood, or **Maren Anna** in Sørvågen, which offers traditional Norwegian dishes.

For those staying at **Svinøya Rorbuer**, you're close to the Lofoten War Museum in Svolvær, which provides fascinating insights into the region's history during World War II. Another must-do is taking a boat tour to see the Trollfjord, a dramatic and narrow fjord with stunning cliffs. For dining, **Børsen Spiseri** in Svinøya offers a gourmet experience with local ingredients, and **Du Verden** in Svolvær provides a more casual dining option with great views of the harbor.

You'll wake up to the sound of the sea, watch fishing boats as they come and go, and relax on your deck with a hot drink, taking in the serene surroundings.

OUTDOOR ADVENTURES

As you may know already the top hiking spot, start with the **Reinebringen hike** near the village of Reine on Moskenesøya. The trail is about 2 kilometers round trip and takes roughly 2 hours to complete. It's steep and challenging, but the view at the top is worth it, with breathtaking panoramas of mountains and fjords. The best time to hike is from May to September. You can park at the designated parking area in Reine. There's no entrance fee, and the trail is open all day. Wear sturdy hiking shoes, bring water, snacks, and a camera for the amazing views.

Another fantastic hiking spot is **Kvalvika Beach**. The trail to this secluded beach is moderate, about 4 kilometers round trip, and takes around 2 hours. Start from the parking lot at Torsfjord near Fredvang. The best time to visit is in the summer when the weather is mild. There's no entrance fee, and the trail is open all day.

For fishing, head to **Å i Lofoten** at the southern tip of Moskenesøya. Drive along the E10 highway to reach this village known for its rich fishing grounds. Join a local fishing tour like **Å Rorbuer Fishing Tours**, which provide all the gear and guidance you need. The best fishing season is from February to April, during the cod season. Tours typically start from 600 NOK per person and run throughout the day. Dress warmly, as it can be chilly on the water, and bring gloves and a hat.

If kayaking is your thing, the waters around **Henningsvær** are perfect. Henningsvær is on Austvågøya, reachable by driving along the E10 and taking the exit towards Henningsvær. Rent kayaks from **Lofoten Aktiv** in the village. The calm, clear waters around the islands make for a peaceful kayaking experience. The best time for kayaking is from June to August. Rentals usually start at 400 NOK for half a day. Wear a waterproof jacket, bring a dry bag for your belongings.

For accommodation, staying in a rorbu cabin is ideal. **Eliassen Rorbuer** in Hamnøy is great if you plan to hike and fish. Located on Moskenesøya, it's accessible via the E10 highway from Moskenes or Å. Prices start at around 1,500 NOK per night. These cabins offer stunning views of the fjord and mountains, perfect for relaxing after a day of exploring. Check-in is from 3 PM, and check-out is by 11 AM. Services include free parking, Wi-Fi, a restaurant on-site, and bike rentals.

Svinøya Rorbuer in Svolvær is excellent for kayaking. These cabins are on a small island connected to Svolvær by a bridge, offering easy access to the town's amenities and a secluded feel. Prices also start around 1,500 NOK per night. The cabins have cozy wooden interiors and views of the harbor. Drive along the E10 and follow the signs to Svolvær. Check-in is from 2 PM, and check-out is by 12 PM. Services include a restaurant, Wi-Fi, guided tours, and fishing trips.

To prepare for these outdoor adventures, pack layers to stay warm and dry, sturdy footwear for hiking, and any personal fishing or kayaking gear you prefer. Bring snacks, water, and a first aid kit. Always check the weather forecast before heading out and let someone know your plans.

While staying at **Eliassen Rorbuer**, visit the village of Å and explore the Norwegian Fishing Village Museum, open from 10 AM to 5 PM with tickets costing 100 NOK. After hiking or fishing, enjoy a meal at **Anitas Sjømat** in Sakrisøy for fresh seafood or **Maren Anna** in Sørvågen for traditional Norwegian cuisine.

If you're at **Svinøya Rorbuer**, visit the Lofoten War Museum in Svolvær, open from 9 AM to 6 PM with tickets costing 120 NOK. Consider a boat tour to Trollfjord, known for its dramatic cliffs, with tours typically costing around 800 NOK per person and lasting about 3 hours. For dining, **Børsen Spiseri** in Svinøya offers a gourmet experience with local ingredients, while **Du Verden** in Svolvær provides a casual setting with great harbor views.

6 TROMSØ

This city has a fascinating history that dates back to the 13th century when it started as a small fishing village. Over the years, it became an important center for Arctic hunting and exploration, earning the nickname "Gateway to the Arctic." Explorers like Roald Amundsen and Fridtjof Nansen began their polar expeditions from this city, giving it a significant place in history. The city's role in these expeditions solidified its reputation as a crucial starting point for Arctic adventures, attracting explorers and scientists eager to delve into the mysteries of the polar regions.

This northern city is renowned for its stunning natural beauty and the beautiful cultural scene. Located about 350 kilometers north of the Arctic Circle, it is surrounded by fjords, mountains, and islands, making it an ideal destination for who want adventure or tranquility. With a population of around 75,000 and covering an area of 2,558 square kilometers, it's one of the largest cities in northern Norway. The unique geographical position allows tourists to experience phenomena like the Northern Lights and the Midnight Sun, which are rare and captivating.

What sets this place apart is its location, offering some of the best views of the Northern Lights from September to April. The Midnight Sun from May to July provides endless daylight, perfect for outdoor activities. This combination of natural wonders and cultural richness makes Tromsø a destination where you can hike rugged mountains during the day.

The **Arctic Cathedral**, built in 1965, is a must. Its striking architecture and beautiful stained-glass windows make it an iconic landmark. The cathedral also hosts concerts throughout the year, adding to its cultural appeal. The design, inspired by the natural surroundings of the Arctic region, reflects the beauty and simplicity of the environment, making it a significant architectural and cultural site.

If you are interested in marine life, visit **Polaria**, an Arctic aquarium and visit the center. Here, you can see bearded seals and learn about the Arctic ecosystem through interactive displays and films. It's a great place.

To get a panoramic view of the city, take the **Fjellheisen Cable Car** to Mount Storsteinen. The ride takes just four minutes, and from the top, you can see wonderful views of the city, fjords, and mountains. This spot is especially popular during the Midnight Sun and Northern Lights seasons, offering spectacular photo opportunities. Standing atop Mount Storsteinen, you can take in the sweeping landscapes that define this Arctic region.

The **University of Tromsø**, the world's northernmost university, focuses heavily on Arctic research. The university hosts various events, lectures, and cultural activities throughout the year, contributing to the city's lively atmosphere. The presence of the university fosters a vibrant academic and cultural environment, making this place a hub for innovation and learning in the Arctic.

The **Tromsø Museum** has extensive exhibits on Sami culture, archaeology, and natural history. It's a great place to learn about the indigenous peoples of the region and their history. The museum provides a deep dive into the cultural heritage of the Arctic, offering visitors a comprehensive understanding of the traditions and history that have shaped this unique part of the world.

Don't miss the **Mack Brewery**, the world's northernmost brewery, established in 1877. You can take a tour, learn about its history, and sample unique Arctic beers. The brewery showcases the blend of tradition and innovation that defines this city, giving you a taste of the rich brewing heritage while enjoying the flavors of the Arctic.

CHAPTER 6

BEST SPOTS FOR VIEWING THE NORTHERN LIGHTS

To see the Northern Lights, go to the best spots like Tromsø, the Lofoten Islands, and Svalbard. Visit between September and April when the nights are long and dark. Look for clear skies since clouds can block the view. Check the aurora forecast to pick the best nights.

In Tromsø, head to the Arctic Cathedral area, located at Hans Nilsens veg 41. You can get there by bus number 26 or a short taxi ride. It's open from 10 AM to 6 PM. Another great spot is the top of Mount Storsteinen, which you can reach by taking the Fjellheisen Cable Car. The cable car runs from 10 AM to 11 PM, and tickets cost about 210 NOK for a round trip. From the top, you get amazing views of the city, fjords, and mountains.

In the Lofoten Islands, try Uttakleiv Beach and Haukland Beach. Uttakleiv Beach is on Vestvågøy island and can be reached by driving along the E10 highway. The beach is open all the time and is free to visit. It's far from city lights, making it perfect for seeing the lights. Haukland Beach is nearby and also offers great views. Both beaches are known for their beautiful scenery and reflections of the Northern Lights on the water.

Svalbard is another top location, especially during the polar night from November to January when it's always dark. You can fly to Svalbard Airport from Oslo or Tromsø and then head to Longyearbyen, the main town. Go outside the town to avoid light pollution and get the best views. Svalbard's icy landscape makes the experience even more special.

You can also joing to the local tours to find the best spots. In Tromsø, companies like Arctic Explorers and Chasing Lights offer tours for around 1,200 to 1,500 NOK per person. These tours include transportation and warm drinks. In the Lofoten Islands, Lofoten Lights offers tours for about 1,000 NOK per person. In Svalbard, Better Moments has tours starting around 1,500 NOK per person. These tours take you to the best places to see the lights and often include tips on photography.

WINTER ACTIVITIES

Dog Sledding: For a nice dog sledding experience, head to **Arctic Adventure Tours**, located just outside Tromsø. You can easily reach it by taking a short drive or booking a transfer through the tour provider. Tours typically cost around 1,600 NOK per person and last about 4 hours. They run from early December to late March, with multiple departures daily between 9 AM and 6 PM. When you arrive, you'll meet the huskies and receive instructions on handling the sled. This adventure doesn't require previous experience, and kids over six are usually welcome. Remember to wear warm clothes, water-proof boots, gloves, and a hat to stay comfortable during your ride.

Snowmobiling: For snowmobiling, **Lyngsfjord Adventure** offers guided tours through the stunning Lyngen Alps. Located about an hour and a half drive from Tromsø, you can get there by car or by booking a transfer with the company. Prices for a snowmobile tour are approximately 1,800 NOK per person, and the tours generally last around 7 hours, including transportation. They operate from December to April, with start times typically around 8 AM and 2 PM. You'll begin with a brief training session on operating the snowmobile, then set off on an exhilarating ride through the snowy terrain. Participants need to be at least 18 years old and hold a valid driver's license. Dress warmly in thermal layers, waterproof outerwear, and sturdy boots for the best experience.

Ice Fishing: To try ice fishing, check out **Tromsø Outdoor**, which offers guided ice fishing tours on the frozen lakes around Tromsø. The meeting point is usually at the Tromsø city center, and transportation to the fishing site is included in the tour price, which is around 1,200 NOK per person. Tours run from January to March, typically starting at 10 AM and lasting about 5 hours. You don't need prior experience, as the tour includes all neces-sary gear, such as fishing rods, bait, and ice drills. Make sure to wear warm, waterproof, and insulated clothing to stay comfortable while fishing.

Lyngen Alps for Winter Sports: The Lyngen Alps are a fantastic destina-tion for winter sports like skiing and snowboarding. Located about two hours from Tromsø, you can reach the Lyngen Alps by car or take a bus from Tromsø to Lyngseidet. Several providers in the area offer equipment rentals and lessons, with prices for a full-day rental and lift pass averaging around 700 NOK. The best time for winter sports here is from December to April, with ski lifts typically operating from 9 AM to 4 PM. The facilities include well-maintained slopes, cozy lodges, and hotels where you can stay during your visit.

LOCAL CULTURE

As we discussed before, the Sami people are the indigenous people of northern Norway, Sweden, Finland, and Russia's Kola Peninsula. Their history goes back thousands of years, and they have a strong connection to the Arctic environment. Reindeer herding is a big part of their life, providing food, clothing, and transport. Sami culture is also known for unique handicrafts, or **duodji**, which are made from natural materials like wood, bone, and leather. These items are both useful and decorative, showing off intricate designs and traditional techniques passed down through generations.

You can visit the **Tromsø Museum** at Lars Thørings veg 10 in Tromsø. This museum has many exhibits on Sami history, culture, and their relationship with nature. It's open from 10 AM to 4 PM daily, and the entry fee is 100 NOK. You can get there by taking bus number 34 or 37 from Tromsø city center. At the museum, you'll see traditional Sami clothing, tools, and art that tell the story of their resilient and resourceful lifestyle.

Another important place to visit is the **Sami Center for Contemporary Art** in Karasjok. This center shows modern Sami art and cultural expressions, giving you a look at how Sami traditions are evolving. It's located at Fitnodatgeaidnu 1 and is open from 9 AM to 4 PM on weekdays, with free entry. You can reach it by car or bus from Alta or Kautokeino. The center has a detailed look at contemporary Sami culture and art, with works that mix traditional themes with modern techniques.

If you want a hands-on experience, join a workshop on **duodji**, traditional Sami crafts. These workshops usually cost around 800 NOK per session and teach you how to make items like clothing, tools, and decorations from natural materials. Participating in these workshops gives you hands-on experience with Sami craftsmanship and a deeper understanding of the cultural significance behind each item. For example, the **RiddoDuottarMuseat** in Kautokeino offers such workshops. You can get there by car or bus from Alta. The museum is open from 9 AM to 3 PM on weekdays, with more hours during the tourist season.

If you visit during **Sami Week** in February, you'll experience traditional activities like reindeer racing, yoiking (traditional Sami singing), and handicraft markets. These events are held in Tromsø and provide a vibrant way to experience Sami culture. You can enjoy reindeer races on Storgata and visit the Sami market at the main square. Engaging with locals, enjoying traditional foods, and participating in unique cultural practices offer a deeper insight into Sami life.

The **Sami Parliament** in Karasjok is another key place to learn about Sami culture. This institution provides educational exhibits and resources about the political and social issues affecting the Sami today. It's located at Ávjovárgeaidnu 50 and is open from 8 AM to 3:30 PM on weekdays.

Now, At **Sami Siida**, located about 30 kilometers from Tromsø, you'll have the chance to meet Sami people, learn about the intricacies of reindeer herding, and listen to beautiful stories around a cozy campfire. To get there, you can drive or book a transfer through a tour operator. These tours typically cost around 1,500 NOK per person and are available year-round. The village tour offers an in-depth look at how the Sami live and work in harmony with their environment. You'll get to see the reindeer up close, understand their importance in Sami culture, and perhaps even try your hand at some of the daily tasks involved in herding. The tour usually starts at 10 AM and ends around 4 PM.

Sami Week in February is an ideal time to experience a nice cultural festival that showcases the traditions of the Sami people. Held in Tromsø's city center, this week-long event features a range of activities, including thrilling reindeer races along Storgata, the main street, and enchanting performances of yoiking, which is traditional Sami singing. The festival runs from early morning to late evening, with specific event times posted on the official festival website. You can also visit the bustling Sami market at the main square, where you can purchase beautiful handmade crafts and taste traditional Sami foods. Entry to most events is free, though some activities may have a small fee.

Then, consider joining a **reindeer herding tour**. These tours often include a visit to a Sami family's reindeer camp, typically located in areas like Kautokeino or Karasjok. You can reach these camps by car or by booking a tour that includes transportation. Prices for these tours range from 1,200 to 1,800 NOK per person, and they usually last about 6-8 hours. The tours run from December to April, with a start time around 9 AM. You'll participate in feeding the reindeer and learn about the intricate process of herding.

Traditional music and dance performances are a highlight of any visit to Sami regions. Many cultural centers and festivals feature **yoiking** and traditional dances that are deeply rooted in Sami heritage. For example, at the **Sami Center for Contemporary Art** in Karasjok, located at Fitnodatgeaidnu 1, you can attend performances that blend traditional themes with modern artistic expressions. The center is open from 9 AM to 4 PM on weekdays, and entry is free. Performances are scheduled in the afternoons and evenings, especially during cultural festivals.

Another beautiful experience is participating in a **duodji workshop**, where you can learn the traditional Sami crafts that have been passed down through generations. These workshops are often held at cultural centers like the **RiddoDuottarMuseat** in Kautokeino. Located at Lassiveien 1, the museum is open from 9 AM to 3 PM on weekdays. Workshops usually cost around 800 NOK per session and provide all the materials you'll need. You'll learn to make items like clothing, tools, and decorations using natural materials such as wood, bone, and leather.

In daily life, the Sami people focus a lot on community and family. **Reindeer herding** is a big part of their life. It's not just a job but a way of living that brings people together. They move the herds over long distances to find good grazing lands, which takes a lot of knowledge about the land and weather. Watching or helping with reindeer herding will help you see how important this tradition is.

Traditional clothing called **Gákti** is worn on special occasions. Gákti looks different depending on where a person is from and their family history. These clothes are often decorated with beautiful patterns and silver jewelry, each telling a story about the person's background. When you see these garments at cultural events, you'll notice how proud people are to wear them.

Cultural symbols include the reindeer and the **Sami flag**. The flag has colors representing nature: red for fire, green for nature, yellow for the sun, and blue for the sky. Another important symbol is the **joik**, a unique form of song. Joiking is like telling a story through music about nature and personal experiences. Listening to a joik connects you to a long tradition of storytelling.

Seasonal celebrations are very important. **The Winter Solstice** is a time when people gather to celebrate the return of the sun with traditional foods and stories. It's a time for communities to come together after the long winter. **Sami National Day**, on February 6th, celebrates the first Sami congress in 1917. The day is full of pride and cultural events like parades, traditional foods, and music. **Reindeer calf marking** in the summer is a time when families gather to mark new calves, keeping social bonds strong. This event is also a festive time with food and celebrations.

When meeting locals, always be respectful. Greet them with "Buorre beaivi" (good day). If you are invited to a home or event, dress modestly and follow what others do. If you want to take photos, always ask for permission first. This shows respect for their privacy.

The Sami have a really deep respect for nature. This respect shows in how they use natural resources and care for the land. When you join in their activities, you'll see how they use every part of the reindeer and waste nothing.

7 CULTURAL AND LOCAL LIFE

Norwegian Traditions and Culture

Constitution Day, Celebrated on May 17th, is the most important festival in Norway. It marks the signing of the Norwegian Constitution in 1814. On this day, you'll see parades with children waving flags, people dressed in traditional costumes called **bunad**, and lots of music and dancing. **In Oslo**, the main parade starts at the Royal Palace and travels down Karl Johans gate. Arrive early to get a good spot, as the streets will be packed. Most events are free. Stay in the city center where you can walk to the festivities. **Grand Hotel in Oslo** offers great views of the parades and starts at about 2000 NOK per night.

Midsummer's Eve, or **St. Hans**, is celebrated on June 23rd. This festival marks the summer solstice with bonfires, music, and dancing. **In Stavanger**, celebrations are held at **Møllebukta**, a popular gathering spot. There's no entry fee, and casual, comfortable clothing is best. **Bring a picnic and enjoy the festivities with locals**. To reach Stavanger, fly into Stavanger Airport, Sola, and take a bus or taxi to the city center. Stay in a coastal hotel like **Scandic Stavanger City**, with rates starting at 1200 NOK per night. Enjoy fresh seafood at nearby restaurants like **Fisketorget**.

Bergen International Festival is held in late May and early June, offering music, theater, dance, and visual arts. Artists from around the world perform in venues like Grieghallen and the Bergen National Opera. Tickets range from 200 to 800 NOK, depending on the event. Plan your stay in advance and book tickets early. Bergen is accessible by train, plane, or bus. Stay at **Hotel Norge** in the city center, with rates starting at 1500 NOK per night. Enjoy dining at restaurants like **Lysverket** for a taste of local cuisine. The festival venues are within walking distance from central accommodations.

The Sami Easter Festival in Kautokeino is a vibrant celebration of Sami culture, featuring reindeer racing, joiking (traditional singing), and duodji (handicraft) markets. Held around Easter, the festival offers a unique glimpse into the Sami way of life. Most events are free, but some activities, like reindeer racing, may have a small charge. **Dress warmly**, as Kautokeino can still be cold in the spring. To reach Kautokeino, fly into Alta Airport and take a bus or taxi to Kautokeino. Stay at local accommodations like the **Thon Hotel Kautokeino**, with rates starting at 1100 NOK per night. Try Sami cuisine, such as bidos (reindeer stew), at local eateries. The main events are centered around the **Sami Cultural Center**, a short walk from most accommodations.

Christmas Markets, especially the one in Oslo, are magical in December. These markets are filled with stalls selling crafts, foods, and Christmas decorations. **In Oslo**, visit the market at **Spikersuppa**, located in the city center near Karl Johans gate. Enjoy hot drinks like gløgg (mulled wine) and traditional foods such as pepperkaker (gingerbread cookies). Entry is free, but bring cash for shopping. **Wear warm clothes and comfortable shoes**, as you'll be walking a lot. Stay in a centrally located hotel like the **Radisson Blu Plaza Hotel**, which offers easy access to the market and rates starting at 1600 NOK per night. Nearby attractions like the Oslo Opera House and the Royal Palace are also worth visiting during your stay. The market opens from late November to December 23rd, from 10 AM to 8 PM.

SAMI CULTURE AND REINDEER HERDING

Consider staying in a traditional **Sami tent** or **lavvu** at **Holmen Husky Lodge** near Alta. This lodge offers an authentic Sami experience with reindeer sleigh rides and opportunities to learn about Sami traditions from the people themselves. Prices start at around 2,000 NOK per night. To get there, take a bus or taxi from Alta city center, which is well connected by flights from Oslo and other major cities.

In Inari, Finland, close to the Norwegian border, visit the **Sami Siida Museum**. This museum offers a comprehensive overview of Sami history and culture, with detailed exhibits about the Sami way of life, including seasonal changes and traditional practices. Open daily from 10 AM to 5 PM, the entry fee is 12 EUR. You can reach Inari by driving or taking a bus from Kirkenes, making it a convenient stop if traveling between Norway and Finland.

Book a **Northern Lights tour** with a Sami guide for a unique seasonal experience. Many tours start from Tromsø and head out to less light-polluted areas where you have a higher chance of seeing the aurora borealis. These tours often include traditional Sami storytelling and a warm meal in a lavvu. Prices range from 1,500 to 2,500 NOK per person, and tours typically start around 7 PM and last 5-6 hours. You can book these tours through local operators like **Arctic Guide Service** or **Sami Adventure**.

In the winter, **dog sledding** is another thrilling activity often guided by Sami experts. Learn to harness and drive sled dogs, a skill rooted in traditional Sami knowledge. Tours are available near Tromsø and Alta, costing between 1,200 and 2,000 NOK per person for a half-day excursion. Most tour operators provide warm clothing and gear.

Join a **guided hike** through Sami lands in the summer to learn about traditional uses of local plants and wildlife. These hikes often start from places like Kautokeino or Karasjok and can be booked through local tour companies. Prices for guided hikes range from 800 to 1,500 NOK per person, depending on the duration and specific itinerary.

For a special culinary experience, visit **Restaurant Tinja** in Bardu, where you can enjoy gourmet dishes made from traditional Sami ingredients like reindeer, berries, and fish. The restaurant is open from 5 PM to 10 PM, and prices for a three-course meal start at around 600 NOK. To reach Bardu, drive or take a bus from Narvik or Tromsø.

At Sami Siida, located about 30 kilometers from Tromsø, you can meet Sami people, learn about reindeer herding, and listen to beautiful stories around a cozy campfire. These tours typically cost around 1,500 NOK per person and are available year-round. Drive or book a transfer through a tour operator to get there. The village tour starts at 10 AM and ends around 4 PM, offering an in-depth look at how the Sami live and work in harmony with their environment.

Visiting the **Sami Parliament** in Karasjok, located at Ávjovárgeaidnu 50, provides educational exhibits about the political and social issues affecting the Sami today. Open from 8 AM to 3:30 PM on weekdays, this institution adds a modern perspective to your understanding of Sami culture.

Reindeer herding is a fundamental part of Sami culture, shaping their way of life and traditions for thousands of years. **Reindeer provide food, clothing, and transportation**, making them essential for survival in the Arctic. This practice is about maintaining a deep connection to the land and heritage.

When you visit the Sami community, is important to **respect their traditions**. As i told you before, always greet people with "Buorre beaivi" (good day). If you're invited to join herding activities, **dress warmly and be prepared for physical tasks**. You may need to **ask before taking photos** of people or their property to show respect.

Participating in reindeer herding involves tasks like **feeding the reindeer**, guiding them between grazing areas, and assisting during the calving season. These activities give you a glimpse into the daily life and challenges faced by Sami herders. Winter is a significant time as they prepare the reindeer for harsh Arctic conditions. **Reindeer races** are thrilling events held during this season, showcasing the skill and speed of both animals and their herders.

You can also book a **reindeer herding tour**. These tours, available in places like **Kautokeino** and **Karasjok**, provide an in-depth look at the herding process. Prices typically range from **1,200 to 1,800 NOK per person**, and tours last about **6-8 hours**. Most tours run from **December to April**, starting around **9 AM**. During the tour, you'll learn about the cultural importance of reindeer, participate in daily herding tasks. Tour operators like **Sami Adventure** and **Tromsø Arctic Reindeer** offer these services.

Visiting a **Sami reindeer herding camp** is another alternative. Camps are often located in remote areas, accessible by car or organized tours. Staying at a camp allows you to see firsthand how the Sami live and work in harmony with their environment. You'll observe the seasonal migrations, understand the importance of different grazing lands, and witness the close-knit relationship between the herders and their reindeer. For example, the **Sami Siida Camp** near Tromsø offers such immersive experiences.

The Sami use every part of the reindeer, showcasing their **respect for nature and sustainable practices**. Participating in these practices demonstrates how the Sami have maintained their traditions while adapting to modern challenges. You'll see how nothing goes to waste, with every part of the reindeer used for food, clothing, tools, and art.

To get to these locations, you can fly into **Alta Airport** and take a bus or taxi to Kautokeino or Karasjok. Many tours offer transportation as part of the package, making it easier to reach the remote herding camps. You may need to **book your accommodations in advance**, as places can fill up quickly during peak seasons. Staying in a traditional **lavvu** or local guesthouse adds to the authenticity of your experience. For example, **Thon Hotel Kautokeino** provides comfortable lodging with easy access to herding activities.

TRADITIONAL MUSIC AND DANCE

To experience the **traditional Norwegian music and dance**, start visiting those interesting places and events.

First, head to the **National Folk Music Festival** in Førde. This festival happens every July and is where you can hear the enchanting sounds of the **Hardanger fiddle**. Tickets usually cost around 400 NOK per day. To get there, fly into Førde Airport and take a short taxi ride to the festival venue. Performances start in the late afternoon and continue into the evening, so you have plenty of time to enjoy the music.

For a more intimate setting, visit the **Norwegian Folk Museum** in Oslo at Museumsveien 10. Open daily from 10 AM to 5 PM, the entry fee is 160 NOK. The museum regularly hosts live music performances, especially in the summer. Here, you can listen to traditional tunes played on the Hardanger fiddle and other folk instruments. Take bus number 30 from Oslo city center, and it will drop you right at the entrance.

If you're interested in dance, don't miss a performance of the **Halling** dance, known for its high kicks and acrobatic moves. Visit **Riksscenen** in Oslo, located at Trondheimsveien 2. This venue is dedicated to folk music and dance, and it's open from Tuesday to Saturday, with performances starting at 7 PM. Tickets cost around 250 NOK. Reach Riksscenen by taking tram number 11 or 12 to Schous Plass.

The **Telemark Festival** in Bø, held every July, is another excellent opportunity to experience traditional music and dance. Known for its vibrant performances and interactive workshops, tickets range from 300 to 600 NOK. To get to Bø, take a train from Oslo, which takes about three hours. The festival features outdoor and indoor stages with performances running throughout the day and evening. Workshops often need advance registration, so check the festival's website for details.

For a deeper Norway's folk music traditions, visit the **Setesdal Valley**. This area is famous for its rich cultural heritage, and you can explore several cultural centers and museums. The **Setesdal Museum** in Rysstad, located at Setesdalsvegen 3475, is open from 10 AM to 5 PM during the summer, with an entry fee of 100 NOK. Drive or take a bus from Kristiansand, about three hours away. The museum offers exhibits on local history and hosts live performances of traditional music.

Check the schedule at the **Norwegian National Opera and Ballet** in Oslo, located at Kirsten Flagstads Plass 1. This venue occasionally hosts performances that feature traditional Norwegian music and dance. The schedule and ticket prices vary, so i suggest you to check their website for details.

Another excellent destination is the **Hallingdal Museum** in Nesbyen. Located at Museumsvegen 1, it's open from 10 AM to 4 PM, and the entry fee is 120 NOK. It's accessible by train or bus from Oslo, taking about two hours. The museum offers demonstrations of traditional dances and music, and you can learn about the history and significance of these cultural expressions. Special events and performances are often scheduled.

Knut Buen and **Annbjørg Lien** are notable musicians you should know. Knut is a master of the Hardanger fiddle, while Annbjørg is famous for her innovative interpretations of traditional music. They often perform at festivals and cultural events, providing you the chance to hear some traditional music live.

8 CUISINE

MUST-TRY DISHES

Brunost, or brown cheese, is a staple in Norwegian cuisine that you absolutely must try. This caramel-colored cheese has a slightly sweet taste and is often enjoyed on slices of bread or crispbread. For a truly authentic experience, visit **Mathallen Food Hall** in Oslo. Here, you can sample different varieties of brunost and learn about its preparation. Mathallen is located at Vulkan 5 and is open from 10 AM to 8 PM on weekdays and from 10 AM to 6 PM on weekends. You can reach Mathallen by taking tram number 11 or bus number 54 to the Olaf Ryes Plass stop, then walking about 10 minutes. Prices for brunost range from 30 to 100 NOK depending on the type and brand.

Rakfisk, a traditional dish made from fermented fish, is a unique part of Norwegian culinary heritage. This dish is usually prepared from trout or char, which is salted and left to ferment for several months. To try rakfisk, head to **Valdres**, a region known for its high-quality rakfisk production. The **Rakfisk Festival** held annually in Fagernes is the perfect place to taste and purchase this delicacy. The festival typically occurs in early November, and entry fees are around 150 NOK. Outside of the festival, you can find rakfisk at **Munkekroen Restaurant** in Fagernes, located at Jernbanevegen 25.

Munkekroen is open from 11 AM to 10 PM. To reach Fagernes, you can take a bus from Oslo, which takes about 3.5 hours.

Lutefisk is another must-try, though it can be polarizing due to its unique texture and preparation method. This dish is made from dried cod that has been soaked in a lye solution, then rehydrated and rinsed thoroughly before cooking. The result is a jelly-like consistency that is often served with boiled potatoes, mashed peas, bacon, and mustard. **Bergen** and **Trondheim** are great places to find restaurants specializing in lutefisk. **To Kokker** in Bergen, located in Bryggen, offers a traditional lutefisk dinner during the Christmas season. To Kokker is located at Enhjørningsgården 29 and is open from 5 PM to 11 PM. Prices for a lutefisk meal typically range from 350 to 500 NOK. You can reach To Kokker by taking a bus or tram to the Bryggen stop, then walking a short distance. Reservations are recommended, especially during the holiday season.

For a broader taste of Norwegian cuisine, visit **Engebret Café** in Oslo, the oldest restaurant in the city. Located at Bankplassen 1, Engebret Café serves a variety of traditional dishes, including many mentioned here. The restaurant is open from 11 AM to 10 PM, and it's wise to make a reservation, especially during peak dining hours. Prices for main courses range from 200 to 400 NOK. You can reach Engebret Café by taking tram number 12 to the Christiania Torv stop.

DINING ETIQUETTE

Norwegians typically eat three main meals a day: breakfast, lunch, and dinner. Breakfast is usually a light meal that might include bread with cheese or cold cuts, cereal, or yogurt. Lunch is often a simple affair, sometimes just a sandwich, while dinner, served between 5 PM and 7 PM, is the main meal of the day and usually involves more elaborate dishes.

In restaurants, it's normal to seat yourself unless there's a host to guide you. **Make sure to greet the staff with a polite "hei" or "god dag"** when you enter. If you're not sure about something on the menu, ask the waiter for explanations or recommendations, they will be very happy to help you. It's common to drink water with your meal, which is usually served for free.

Tipping practices are a bit different. Service charges are included in the bill, so tipping isn't mandatory. However, it's customary to **round up the bill**

or leave a **5-10% tip** if you're particularly pleased with the service. For instance, if your bill is 270 NOK, rounding up to 300 NOK is a nice gesture.

Reservations are recommended for dinner, especially at popular or fine dining restaurants. You can make reservations online or by phone. When you make a reservation, be punctual; they value timeliness. If you're running late, as you may know already, it's polite to call the restaurant and inform them.

When it's time to **pay the bill**, signal the waiter by making eye contact or raising your hand slightly. Ask for the bill by saying "Kan jeg få regningen, takk?" (Can I have the bill, please?). In most places, you can pay by card, and it's common to use contactless payments. If you're dining with others, it's perfectly acceptable to ask for separate checks, or you can split the bill evenly.

Norwegian dining customs emphasize a relaxed and respectful atmosphere. People tend to eat at a leisurely pace, enjoying their food and conversation. **Eating slowly and savoring each bite** is part of the dining culture. It's also polite to keep your hands visible, resting your wrists on the table rather than your elbows.

When dining out, you might encounter some **special dining traditions**, particularly during holidays. For example, during Christmas, many Norwegians enjoy a festive meal of pinnekjøtt (dried lamb ribs) or ribbe (roast pork belly) with family and friends. If you're invited to a Norwegian home for dinner, it's a good idea to bring a small gift, such as flowers or chocolates, and to remove your shoes at the door.

Norwegian menu can be straightforward, but here are some tips: look for familiar words or dishes you've heard of, and don't be afraid to ask help for a recommendation. Main courses are listed under "Hovedretter," appetizers under "Forretter," and desserts under "Dessert."

Handling common dining situations is easy if you follow these guidelines. For breakfast and lunch, self-service is common, especially in cafes and casual eateries. For dinner, service is usually more formal.

FOOD MARKETS AND RESTAURANTS

You must visit the best food markets and top restaurants. **Mathallen Food Hall** in Oslo is an essential stop.

Located at Vulkan 5, it's open from 10 AM to 8 PM on weekdays and from 10 AM to 6 PM on weekends. Here, you can try local food like cured meats, cheeses, and fresh seafood. Try the **reindeer sausages** and **smoked salmon**. For dessert,the **Skillingsboller**, a Norwegian cinnamon bun. To get there, take tram number 11 or bus number 54 to the Olaf Ryes Plass stop, then walk about 10 minutes. Prices vary, but you can expect to spend around 50 to 200 NOK per item.

Next, head to **Bergen's Fish Market**, located at Torget in the city center. Open daily from 7 AM to 10 PM during the summer months, this market is brimming with fresh seafood and local delicacies. Try fish soup and shrimp sandwiches right by the water. Make sure to try **persetorsk**, a traditional Bergen specialty of pressed cod. For a sweet treat, look for **Kvæfjordkake**, also known as the world's best cake. The market is accessible by foot from most parts of downtown Bergen.

For a nice dining in Oslo, visit **Smalhans** at Ullevålsveien 43. This restaurant serves locally sourced dishes in a cozy, rustic setting. Open from 4 PM to 10 PM on weekdays and from 12 PM to 10 PM on weekends, Smalhans offers main courses ranging from 200 to 400 NOK. Try their **slow-cooked lamb** or **baked cod**. For dessert, their **chocolate fondant** is highly recommended. You can get there by taking tram number 17 or 18 to the St. Hanshaugen stop.

In Trondheim, **Credo** is a top restaurant renowned for its Michelin-starred Nordic cuisine. Located at Ladeveien 9, it's open from Wednesday to Saturday, 6 PM to 11 PM. Reservations are essential, and a tasting menu can cost up to 2000 NOK. Their tasting menu changes seasonally but often includes dishes like **langoustine with seaweed** and **fermented vegetables**. For dessert, you might find a creative twist on traditional flavors, like **cloudberry sorbet**. To reach Credo, take bus number 6 to the Lade stop, then walk about 5 minutes.

If you're in Stavanger, visit **Fisketorget** at Strandkaien 37. This market, open from 10 AM to 10 PM, offers fresh seafood and local produce. It's the perfect place to sample **klippfisk** (dried and salted cod) and **lutefisk**. Nearby small eateries prepare these dishes to perfection. For a sweet finish, try **Multekrem**, a dessert made from cloudberries and whipped cream. The market is easy to find and walkable from the main city center.

Food festivals are a great way to dive into the local cuisine. The **Gladmat Festival** in Stavanger, held every July, is Scandinavia's largest food festival. It features food stalls, cooking demonstrations, and tastings. Entry is free, but prices for food and drinks vary. Look out for **fish cakes** and **brown cheese ice cream** among the numerous stalls.

If you are Vegetarian or Vegan, **Nordvegan** in Oslo is fantastic. Located at Kristian IVs gate 15, it's open from 11 AM to 9 PM. This restaurant offers a diverse menu, including vegan versions of traditional Norwegian dishes like **vegan stew** and **plant-based burgers**. Another great spot is **Happolati** at St. Olavs plass 2, serving creative vegetarian dishes from 5 PM to 11 PM, Tuesday to Saturday. Try their **grilled vegetable platter** and **chickpea pancakes**.

In Bergen, **Daily Pot** provides delicious vegetarian and vegan bowls. Located at Kong Oscars gate 18, it's open from 11 AM to 6 PM. The menu changes daily and features fresh, local ingredients, ensuring a healthy dining experience. Their **vegan Buddha bowl** and **quinoa salad** are particularly popular. So, why don't try it!

9 ACCOMODATIONS AROUND NORWAY

Hotels offer options for different budgets. If you are on budget, i suggest you to stay at **Citybox Oslo**, where you get clean rooms and free Wi-Fi. Located near the city center, you can easily reach it by tram number 11 or bus number 54 to Olaf Ryes Plass, then a 10-minute walk. Rooms cost between 500 and 900 NOK per night. For more comfort, consider **Thon Hotel Rosenkrantz** in Bergen, with modern rooms, a fitness center, and a breakfast buffet, priced around 1,200 NOK per night. It's located at Rosenkrantzgaten 7 and within walking distance to Bryggen Wharf and the Fish Market. If you want luxury, the **Grand Hotel** in Oslo offers elegant rooms and spa services, starting at 2,500 NOK per night, located right on Karl Johans gate.

Hostels are great if you're on a budget or enjoy meeting people. **Anker Hostel** in Oslo offers both dorms and private rooms. It's centrally located at Storgata 55 and can be reached by tram number 11 or bus number 30. Dorm beds start at 300 NOK, private rooms at 700 NOK. You'll find a communal kitchen to prepare your meals, saving you money on food. Nearby attractions include the Oslo Opera House and Munch Museum.

Cabins provide a cozy stay, especially in the countryside or fjord regions. They range from basic shelters to modern accommodations with full kitchens.

The **rorbuer cabins** in the Lofoten Islands are traditional fishermen's cabins with beautiful waterfront views, starting at 1,500 NOK per night. They're perfect if you like the nature. You can reach these cabins by flying into Leknes Airport and taking a taxi or rental car. Nearby activities include fishing, hiking, and boat tours.

For a beautiful experiences, try **special accommodations** like treehouses, yurts, or ice hotels. The **Kirkenes Snowhotel** in Northern Norway offers rooms made of snow and ice, with thermal sleeping bags to keep you warm. Prices start at 2,500 NOK per night. This stay are incredible and includes intricately carved ice sculptures. You have to dress warmly and follow the guidelines. It's located near the Russian border, and you can reach it by flying into Kirkenes Airport and taking a shuttle service. Nearby attractions include husky sledding and Northern Lights tours.

Boutique hotels offer a more personalized visit. **Hotel Brosundet** in Ålesund is located at Apotekergata 5 and offers stylish rooms with sea views, priced around 1,500 NOK per night. You can reach it by flying into Ålesund Airport and taking a bus or taxi. Nearby, you can visit the Atlantic Sea-Park and take a stroll through the Art Nouveau district.

In the end, you can try the **Juvet Landscape Hotel** in Valldal, where modern architecture blends with nature, offering stunning views. Rooms start at 2,200 NOK per night. It's located about 90 minutes from Ålesund by car. You can visit the nearby Gudbrandsjuvet gorge and the Geirangerfjord.

Or stay at the historic **Stiftsgården** in Trondheim, which provides a taste of Norwegian history and charm, with prices starting at 1,800 NOK per night. It's located at Munkegata 23 and easily reachable by bus from Trondheim Airport. The Nidaros Cathedral and Bakklandet neighborhood are just a short walk away.

Camping sites are ideal if you like the outdoors. **Preikestolen Camping** near Stavanger offers both tents and cabins, with prices starting at 300 NOK per night for a tent site and 800 NOK for a cabin. You can reach it by car or bus from Stavanger. Nearby, you can hike to the famous Preikestolen (Pulpit Rock).

Luxury Stays

If you want top-notch service and amenities, the **Grand Hotel** in Oslo is perfect. Located on Karl Johans gate, it offers elegantly decorated rooms, a luxurious spa, and fine dining. Prices start at 2,500 NOK per night. You'll love the rooftop bar with beautiful city views. The Grand Hotel is near the Royal Palace and the National Gallery. Reach it by taking tram number 11 or bus number 54 to the Nationaltheatret stop, and it's a short walk from there.

In **Bergen**, the **Hotel Norge by Scandic** offers stylish rooms and a wellness area. Rooms start around 2,200 NOK per night. Located at Nedre Ole Bulls Plass 4, it's in the heart of Bergen, close to Bryggen Wharf and the Fish Market. Reach the hotel by taking the airport shuttle to the Bergen Bus

Station and then a short walk. Make reservations early to secure your stay at this popular hotel.

Another luxury option in **Tromsø** is the **Radisson Blu Hotel**, which provides panoramic views of the fjords and mountains. Located at Sjøgata 7, the hotel offers a sauna and a rooftop terrace. Rooms start at 2,300 NOK per night. You can easily reach the hotel from Tromsø Airport by taking the Flybussen service. Nearby attractions include the Polar Museum and the Arctic Cathedral.

Mid-Range

For a comfortable and affordable stay at the same time, choose the **Thon Hotel Rosenkrantz** in Bergen. This hotel, situated at Rosenkrantzgaten 7, offers modern rooms and a great breakfast buffet. Rooms are priced around 1,200 NOK per night. This location is excellent for exploring Bryggen Wharf and Mount Fløyen. Booking directly through the hotel's website often includes breakfast and provides the best rates. So, why not!

In **Oslo**, **Scandic Victoria** is a good mid-range option. Located at Rosenkrantz' gate 13, it offers modern amenities and a central location. Rooms start at 1,300 NOK per night. You'll be close to the Oslo Opera House and Aker Brygge. Take tram number 11 to the Nationaltheatret stop and walk from there.

In Trondheim, the **Comfort Hotel Park** at Prinsens gate 4A is a great mid-range choice. With rooms starting at 1,100 NOK per night, it offers comfortable accommodations and is conveniently located near the Nidaros Cathedral and the Old Town Bridge. Reach the hotel by taking a bus from Trondheim Airport to the city center.

Budget Options

If you are a budget-conscious tourist, **Citybox Oslo** provides you a clean, affordable rooms with free Wi-Fi. Located at Prinsens gate 6, it's a 10-minute walk from the Olaf Ryes Plass tram stop. Rooms cost between 500 and 900 NOK per night. It's a great base for exploring Oslo without breaking the bank. Nearby, visit the Oslo Opera House and the Munch Museum.

Another excellent hotel is then**Anker Hostel** in Oslo, located at Storgata

55. It offers dormitory-style and private rooms. Dorm beds start at 300 NOK, and private rooms at 700 NOK. The hostel has a communal kitchen, which helps you save on dining costs. Around you can visit the Oslo Opera House and the Munch Museum. It's easily accessible by tram number 11 or bus number 30.

In **Bergen**, **Bergen Budget Hotel** at Kong Oscars gate 29 offers affordable rooms starting at 600 NOK per night. Is located near the train station, it's an easy walk to Bryggen and the Fish Market. Rooms are simple but clean, making it a good choice. You can reach the hotel by taking the airport shuttle to the Bergen Bus Station and then walking a few minutes.

For a cozy stay, book a **rorbuer cabin** in the Lofoten Islands. These traditional fishermen's cabins offer beautiful waterfront views, starting at 1,500 NOK per night. Fly into Leknes Airport and take a taxi or rental car to reach these cabins. The nearby activities like fishing, hiking, and boat tours. You need to check local tourism websites or Airbnb for the best deals.

If you're looking for something truly unique, the **Kirkenes Snowhotel** in Northern Norway offers rooms made of snow and ice. Prices start at 2,500 NOK per night. The thermal sleeping bags will keep you warm. This hotel is near the Russian border and reachable by flying into Kirkenes Airport and taking a shuttle. Nearby, you can enjoy husky sledding and Northern Lights tours. Book early as availability is limited.

Boutique Hotels

Hotel Brosundet in Ålesund is located at Apotekergata 5 and offers stylish rooms with sea views, priced around 1,500 NOK per night. You can reach it by flying into Ålesund Airport and taking a bus or taxi. Nearby, you can visit the Atlantic Sea-Park and take a stroll through the Art Nouveau district.

Juvet Landscape Hotel in Valldal offers a unique stay with modern architecture and beautiful nature at same time, offering wonderful views. Rooms start at 2,200 NOK per night. It's located about 90 minutes from Ålesund by car. You can visit Gudbrandsjuvet gorge and the Geirangerfjord.

Camping and Outdoor

Preikestolen Camping near Stavanger offers tent sites and cabins. Tent sites start at 300 NOK per night, and cabins at 800 NOK. The campsite is perfect for hiking to Preikestolen (Pulpit Rock). Reach it by car or bus from Stavanger. Around you can find breathtaking hikes and wonderful fjord views.

Budget Hotels in Smaller Towns

In Geiranger, consider the **Havila Hotel Geiranger**. Located at Geirangervegen 22, it offers budget-friendly rooms starting at 900 NOK per night with views of the fjord. Reach the hotel by car or bus from Ålesund. It's a great position to explore the Geirangerfjord and taking boat tours.

In Flam, the **Flamsbrygga Hotel** offer rooms starting at 1,200 NOK per night. Located at A-Feltvegen 7, it's near the Flam Railway and the fjord. Reach the hotel by train from Oslo or Bergen. Around, you can enjoy fjord cruises and the scenic railway journey.

10 OUTDOOR ADVENTURES

HIKING AND TREKKING

Firstup, **Besseggen Ridge** in Jotunheimen National Park. **You start your experience at Gjendesheim Turisthytte**, which is accessible by a direct bus from Oslo to Gjendesheim. The bus ride takes approximately 5 hours. The hike itself is about 14 kilometers long and is rated from moderate to challenging, typically taking 6-8 hours to complete. The best time to hike Besseggen is from late June to early September. **The trailhead is open from 7 AM to 9 PM during the hiking season.** You'll be treated to spectacular views of the emerald green Gjende lake and the deep blue Bessvatnet lake. **There is no entrance fee to the park, but you might need to pay for parking if you arrive by car.**

Next, there's **Trolltunga** in Odda. **To get there, take a bus from Odda to the Skjeggedal trailhead**, which is about a 20-minute ride. This hike is strenuous, spanning approximately 28 kilometers round trip and taking about 10-12 hours. The best time to hike Trolltunga is from mid-June to mid-September. **The trailhead is accessible from 7 AM to 10 PM during the hiking season.** The famous Trolltunga rock formation juts out over the valley below, providing a breathtaking photo opportunity. Start early in the morning, bring plenty of water, food, and warm clothing. The weather can change quickly, so be prepared. There is no fee for hiking Trolltunga, but guided tours are available at varying prices.

For something a bit easier, try the **Preikestolen (Pulpit Rock) hike near Stavanger**. **The trailhead is at Preikestolen Fjellstue, which you can reach by taking a ferry from Stavanger to Tau and then a bus to the trailhead.** This journey takes around an hour and a half. The hike is about 8 kilometers round trip and takes approximately 4-5 hours to complete. **The best time to hike is from April to October, with the trailhead open from 8 AM to 8 PM.** The view from the top, overlooking the Lysefjord, is simply breathtaking. **There is no entrance fee to hike Preikestolen, but parking costs around 250 NOK.**

If you want something less crowded, **Romsdalseggen Ridge near Åndalsnes** is perfect. **Begin your hike at Venjesdalen, accessible by bus from Åndalsnes, which is about a 20-minute ride.** The hike is about 10 kilometers long and takes around 6-7 hours to complete. **The best time to hike Romsdalseggen is from June to September, with the trailhead open from 7 AM to 9 PM during the hiking season.** The ridge offers breathtaking views of the surrounding mountains and fjords, including the famous Trollveggen (Troll Wall). **There is no entrance fee for this hike, and parking is free at the trailhead.**

Then, try hiking in the **Lofoten Islands**. The **Reinebringen** hike starts from the village of Reine. **You can get there by flying into Leknes Airport and then taking a bus or taxi to Reine.** The hike is about 2 kilometers round trip but is quite steep and demanding due to the elevation gain. **The best time to hike Reinebringen is from May to September, with the trailhead accessible from 6 AM to 10 PM during the hiking season.** From the top, you will have beautidul views over the Reinefjorden and the surrounding peaks. There is no fee to hike Reinebringen, but guided tours are available for those who prefer a more structured experience.

WILDLIFE WATCHING

For **whale watching**, head to **Andenes** in the Vesterålen archipelago. **You can fly into Andenes Airport from Oslo or take a ferry from the mainland.** The best time to see whales, like sperm whales, humpback whales, and orcas, is from May to September. **Tours usually start around 9 AM and run until late** afternoon, costing between 900 to 1,500 NOK per person. You have to dress warmly in layers and bring waterproof clothing since it can get cold and wet out on the boat.

If you want like bird watching, the **Varanger Peninsula** is a must. **Fly into Kirkenes Airport, then drive to Varanger.** The best time to visit is from May to July during the breeding season. **You'll see seabirds like puffins, king eiders, and sea eagles.** Varanger Bird Park offers guided tours starting at 8 AM for around 700 NOK per person. **Pack binoculars, a good camera with a zoom lens, and a field manual to identify the birds will be a great idea.**

For **reindeer watching**, go to **Finnmark**, especially around Kautokeino and Karasjok. **Fly into Alta Airport and drive to these towns.** The best time to see reindeer is during the winter from December to March when they stand out against the snow. **Local Sami guides offer tours starting around 1,200 NOK per person.** The tours usually begin at 9 AM and include transportation, warm clothing, and sometimes a meal. **Respect the reindeer and follow the guide's instructions to avoid stressing the animals.**

When wildlife watching, keep a safe distance and never try to feed or touch the animals. **Binoculars and a good camera are needed to catch the view.** Dress in layers, wear waterproof and windproof outerwear, and sturdy boots. Bring also some snacks and water since you might be out for several hours.

SKIING AND SNOWBOARDING

The first is **Trysil**, the largest ski resort in Norway. Is **located about 2.5 hours from Oslo, you can get there by taking a direct bus or driving.** When you arrive, you'll find a well-equipped resort with everything from rental equipment to cozy lodges. **The best time to visit Trysil is from December to April.** The resort boasts a wide variety of trails suitable for all levels, from beginners slopes to advanced runs. **Lift passes start at around 400 NOK per day, and equipment rentals cost about 300 NOK per day.** Trysil also offers nice facilities, including many ski schools where all the beginners can take lessons. Expect to find modern lifts, well-groomed trails, and a friendly atmosphere.

Next, we have **Hemsedal**, known as the Scandinavian Alps. **Hemsedal is about a 3-hour drive from Oslo, and regular buses run from the city.** This resort is famous for its diverse terrain, offering 50 slopes that cater to all skill levels. **The best time to visit Hemsedal is from November to May.** Here, lift passes are priced around 450 NOK per day, and renting equipment will cost you about 350 NOK per day. The resort offers night skiing, which is a wonderful experience under the lights. Alos here if you are beginners you will find many ski schools that will provide you excellent instruction, ensuring you get the hang of skiing or snowboarding quickly.

If you prefer a quieter spot, consider **Myrkdalen** near Voss. **You can reach it by driving about 2 hours from Bergen, or by taking a train to Voss and then a bus to Myrkdalen.** This resort is perfect for who is looking to avoid crowds. **The best time to visit Myrkdalen is from December to April.** Lift passes cost around 400 NOK per day, and equipment rentals are about 300 NOK per day. The resort offers great powder snow and a variety of trails. You'll find dedicated areas for learning and more challenging runs for those with experience.

If you are more adventurous, **Røldal** is a hidden gem. **Located about 3.5 hours from Bergen, you can drive or take a bus.** Røldal is renowned for its deep snow and excellent off-piste opportunities. **The best time to visit Røldal is from November to April.** Lift passes here are around 400 NOK per day, and rental equipment costs about 350 NOK per day. This resort is ideal for experienced skiers and snowboarders looking for a challenge. The terrain offers steep slopes and plenty of off-piste areas to explore. Guided tours for off-piste skiing are available, costing around 800 NOK and including safety equipment like avalanche transceivers.

When you plan the trip, pack the right gear. **Dress in layers to stay warm and dry, and ensure you have waterproof clothing.** Helmets is necessary for safety, and good-quality goggles as you may already know to protect your eyes from the snow glare. If you're renting equipment, try to arrive early to avoid long lines.

11 STAYING SAFE AND HEALTHY

UNDERSTANDING TRAVEL INSURANCE

Travel insurance is super important when you're planning your trip. **It's your safety net for unexpected things like medical emergencies, trip cancellations, or lost luggage.** When you choose a policy, make sure it covers the basics: **medical expenses, trip cancellations, interruptions, lost or stolen belongings, and emergency evacuations.**

You should also look for coverage that includes any outdoor activities you plan to do. **For example, if you're hiking or skiing, check that these activities are covered. Travel insurance usually costs about 4-10% of your total trip cost.**

World Nomads, Allianz, and Travel Guard are popular providers. You can buy your policy online. Just visit their websites, compare the plans, and pick the one that fits your needs. Enter your trip details and personal information to complete the purchase.

Read the policy details carefully. Make sure you understand what's covered and what isn't. Pay special attention to exclusions, which are things the policy won't cover. For example, some policies don't cover pre-existing medical conditions or certain high-risk activities. Knowing this helps avoid surprises if you need to make a claim.

If you need to file a claim, keep all your receipts and documents. Insurance providers need proof of the expenses you're claiming, like medical bills or receipts for items you had to replace. Contact your insurance provider right away to start the claims process. They'll guide you through the steps, which usually involve filling out a claim form and submitting it with your supporting documents.

To find the best deals, **compare different providers and policies.** Is a good idea to buy insurance as soon as you book your trip to get coverage for cancellations. Check in order to have enough coverage, especially if you plan to do activities like skiing or hiking, which might need extra coverage.

EMERGENCY CONTACTS

For police assistance, dial 112. If you need urgent help from the police, this is the number you call. **When you call, make sure you provide your location, a brief description of the emergency, and your contact details.** Staying calm and speaking clearly will help the operator understand your situation and send help quickly.

For medical emergencies, dial 113. This connects you directly to emergency medical services, including ambulances. **Clearly state your location, the nature of the medical emergency, and any important information about the person's condition, like allergies or ongoing treatments.** Having this information ready helps the responders assist you faster.

If you need to contact your embassy, search online for the contact details of your country's embassy in Norway. Each embassy usually has a 24-hour emergency number for citizens. **Save this number in your phone before you travel.** If you lose your passport or need urgent assistance, your embassy can help with legal issues, replacement travel documents, and advice on local resources.

12 MUST ATTRACTIONS AND ACTIVITIES

3-DAY ITINERARY

Day 1 Oslo

Start in **Oslo** with a visit to the **Viking Ship Museum** on the Bygdøy Peninsula. **This museum has amazing Viking ships and artifacts.** It is open daily from 10 AM to 4 PM, and the entrance fee is **120 NOK**. Take bus number 30 from the city center, a **20-minute ride** costing **37 NOK**.

Next, go to the **Royal Palace**. You can tour the palace in summer for **135 NOK** and see the changing of the guard at 1:30 PM. The palace is a **15-minute walk from the city center**. For lunch, go to **Aker Brygge**, a lively area with lots of restaurants. Try **Lofoten Fiskerestaurant** for fresh seafood, with dishes costing **250 to 400 NOK**.

In the afternoon, visit the **Vigeland Park**, a park with over 200 unique sculptures. The park is always open and free to enter. Then, visit the **Munch Museum** to see Edvard Munch's famous works, like "The Scream." The museum is open from 10 AM to 6 PM, and tickets are **160 NOK**. Take tram line 18 or 19, a **15-minute ride from the city center**.

For dinner, you can check out **Mathallen Oslo**, a food hall with many options, where mains cost **150 to 300 NOK**. Stay at **Hotel Continental** near many attractions. Rooms start at **2,000 NOK per night**. Check-in is at 3 PM, and check-out is at 12 PM.

Day 2 Visit Bergen

Take an early train or flight from Oslo to **Bergen**. The train ride is **7 hours and costs 900 NOK**, or fly in **1 hour** for around **500 NOK**. Start your day at **Bryggen Wharf**, a UNESCO World Heritage site. Visit the **Hanseatic Museum** from 10 AM to 4 PM for **100 NOK**. For lunch, go to the **Fish Market**, open daily from 7 AM to 10 PM.

In the afternoon, take the **Fløibanen funicular** to Mount Fløyen. Round-trip tickets are **125 NOK**, and it runs from 7:30 AM to 11 PM. Stay at **Clarion Hotel Admiral** by the harbor, with rooms starting at **1,200 NOK per night**. Check-in at 3 PM, check-out at 12 PM. For dinner, visit **Enhjørningen**, a historic seafood restaurant with mains costing **300 to 500 NOK**.

Day 3 Fjord

Spend your last day visiting the fjords. Take a **fjord cruise from Bergen** for around **600 NOK**, departing at **8 AM** and returning by **6 PM**. For a more , try a **kayak tour** starting at **800 NOK**. Then visit the **Stegastein Viewpoint** for free, open 24 hours, accessible by car or bus.

After that, you have to Return back to Bergen for dinner at **Bryggeloftet & Stuene**, where is offering traditional menu with mains costing **250 to 400 NOK**. Then, spend your last night at **Clarion Hotel Admiral**.

7-DAY ITINERARY

Day 4 Fjord Trip Continues

Begin the fourth day with an early morning drive or bus ride from Bergen to **Geirangerfjord**, which is one of Norway's most famous fjords. If you are driving from Bergen, it will take about six hours and cost roughly **700 NOK** in fuel and tolls, but you can also take a bus for **450 NOK**, which takes around eight hours. Once you arrive, start by visiting the **Geirangerfjord Cruise**, departing at 10 AM and costing **400 NOK**. This cruise lasts about one and a half hours and offers beautiful views of the waterfalls and steep cliffs.

For lunch, you can go to the **Brasserie Posten**, where is located right in Geiranger. This restaurant is known for local dishes like reindeer stew, which costs around **200 NOK**. It is open from 11 AM to 10 PM, providing a nice atmosphere with beautiful views of the fjord.

In the afternoon, take a hike up to the **Flydalsjuvet** viewpoint. This moderate hike takes about two hours round trip and offers spectacular panoramic views. The trail is well-marked and free to access.

For dinner, return to Geiranger and dine at **Westerås Farm**, a good restaurant that have traditional cuisine. Main courses range from **250 to 350 NOK**. It's open from 5 PM to 9 PM, and offers a rustic dining experience with locally sourced ingredients.

Stay overnight at the **Hotel Union Geiranger**, which offers comfortable accommodations with beautiful views of the fjord. Rooms start at **1,500 NOK per night**, with check-in at 3 PM and check-out at 11 AM. This hotel also features a spa.

Day 5 Ålesund and Surroundings

On the fifth day, start from Geiranger to **Ålesund**. If you are driving, the trip takes about two and a half hours and costs around **200 NOK** in fuel, or you can take a bus for **150 NOK**. Start with the **Ålesund Aquarium**, which is open from 10 AM to 5 PM and has an entrance fee of **200 NOK**. This aquarium showcases the marine life of the Norwegian coast.

For lunch, visit **XL Diner**, where is located in the city center. This diner is famous for its bacalao (salted cod), with dishes priced around **250 NOK**. It is open from 12 PM to 10 PM and offers a comfortable dining with a view of the harbor.

Spend the afternoon by visiting the city's **Art Nouveau architecture**. Walk around the city center and visit the **Jugendstilsenteret** (Art Nouveau Center), which is open from 10 AM to 4 PM and charges an entrance fee of **100 NOK**. This center provides an in-depth look at the unique architectural style that defines Ålesund.

For dinner, go to the **Sjøbua Fiskerestaurant**, known for its fresh seafood. Meals here range from **300 to 500 NOK**. It is open from 5 PM to 10 PM and offers a fine dining experience with a focus on local ingredients.

Stay at **Hotel Brosundet**, which offers waterfront views and comfortable accommodations. Rooms start at **1,200 NOK per night**, with check-in at 3 PM and check-out at 12 PM. This hotel combines modern with historical charm, making it an excellent choice for your stay in Ålesund. So i suggest it!

Day 6 Trondheim and Historical Insights

On the sixth day, take an early morning train or flight to **Trondheim**. The train ride takes about five and a half hours and costs **700 NOK**, while a flight is one hour and costs around **500 NOK**. Begin the day in Trondheim by visiting the **Nidaros Cathedral**, which is open from 9 AM to 3 PM with an entrance fee of **100 NOK**. This beautiful cathedral is a must-see, with its wonderful Gothic architecture and great history.

For lunch, go to the **Bakklandet Skydsstation**, where is located in the historic Bakklandet district. This cozy café is known for its fish soup, priced at **150 NOK**. It is open from 11 AM to 9 PM and offers a comfortable atmosphere with charming décor.

In the afternoon, visit the **Ringve Music Museum**, which is dedicated to musical instruments and the history of music. The museum is open from 11 AM to 4 PM, and tickets cost **120 NOK**. This museum is located in a beautiful manor house.

For dinner, visit **Credo Restaurant**. The menu starts at **1,500 NOK**, offering a variety of dishes using local ingredients. The restaurant is open from 6 PM to 10 PM, providing an elegant setting for a good meal.

Stay overnight at **Scandic Nidelven**, a hotel known for its award-winning breakfast. Rooms start at **1,300 NOK per night**, with check-in at 3 PM and check-out at 12 PM. This hotel is centrally located, making it convenient for visiting the city.

Day 7 Svalbard Adventure

On your final day, fly from Trondheim to **Svalbard** in the morning. The flight takes about three hours and costs around **2,000 NOK**. Upon arrival in **Longyearbyen**, start by visiting with a **dog sledding tour**, which costs **1,200 NOK** and lasts about three hours. This tour offers a good way to visit the Arctic landscape.

For lunch, visit **Fruene**, the northernmost coffee shop in the world. Try their Arctic char sandwich, priced at **180 NOK**. The café is open from 10 AM to 6 PM and provides a cozy spot to warm up and enjoy a meal.

In the afternoon, visit the **Svalbard Museum**, which is open from 10 AM to 5 PM with an entrance fee of **100 NOK**. This museum offers fascinating exhibits on the history and environment of the Svalbard archipelago.

For dinner, dine at **Huset**, which offers a tasting menu featuring Arctic specialties for around **1,000 NOK**. The restaurant is open from 6 PM to 11 PM.

Stay overnight at the **Radisson Blu Polar Hotel**, the world's northernmost full-service hotel. Rooms start at **2,500 NOK per night**, with check-in at 3 PM and check-out at 12 PM. This hotel offers comfortable accommodations, perfect for your last night in Norway. (if is you last day).

14-DAY ITINERARY: CULTURAL AND NATURAL TRIP

Day 8 Trondheim to Røros

You'll start the day with a beautiful train ride from **Trondheim to Røros**, a historic mining town and UNESCO World Heritage Site. The train trip is a beautiful two-hour ride, costing around **250 NOK**. Once you arrive in Røros, explore the **Røros Museum**, located at Malmplassen. This museum is open from 10 AM to 5 PM and has an entrance fee of **100 NOK**. Here, you'll learn about the history of the town and the rich mining heritage.

For lunch, head to **Kaffestuggu**, a charming café known for its hearty traditional dishes like reindeer stew. It's open from 11 AM to 6 PM, and meals here cost around **200 NOK**. The cozy atmosphere makes it a perfect spot to relax.

In the afternoon, stroll through the well-preserved streets of Røros, admiring the wooden buildings that date back to the 17th century. Don't miss the **Røros Church**, an impressive structure and one of the largest wooden buildings in Norway. It's open from 11 AM to 4 PM with an entry fee of **60 NOK**.

For dinner, dine at **Vertshuset Røros**, a fine dining restaurant that focuses on local ingredients and traditional recipes. Open from 6 PM to 10 PM, meals here range from **300 to 500 NOK**. I suggest you to enjoy dishes crafted from locally sourced reindeer, fish, and seasonal vegetables.

You'll spend the night at **Erzscheidergården**, a quaint hotel in the heart of

Røros, where rooms start at **1,200 NOK per night**. Check-in is at 3 PM, and check-out is at 11 AM.

Day 9 Røros to Dovrefjell National Park

Depart Røros early in the morning and head towards **Dovrefjell National Park** by car or bus. The trip takes about two hours and costs around **200 NOK** for fuel or **150 NOK** for a bus ticket. Upon arrival, go to the **Musk Ox Safari**, a nice experience where you can see these animals in their natural habitat. The safari costs around **500 NOK** and lasts about four hours.

For lunch, you have to bring a packed meal or visit the park's café where meals cost about **150 NOK**. Spend the afternoon hiking in the park, choosing from a variety of trails that offer breathtaking views of the mountainous terrain. One recommended trail is the **Snøhetta Viewpoint Trail**, which is moderate and takes about three hours round trip. This trail is free to access.

Return to Røros for dinner at **Bergstadens Hotel Restaurant**, which offers Norwegian dishes priced between **250 and 400 NOK**. The restaurant is open from 5 PM to 9 PM.

Stay another night at **Bergstadens Hotel**, for a restful night with its excellent amenities and convenient location.

Day 10 Dovrefjell to Ålesund

On the tenth day, travel from Dovrefjell to **Ålesund**. If you're driving, the trip takes about four hours and costs around **300 NOK** in fuel. Alternatively, you can take a bus for **200 NOK**, which takes about five hours. Upon arrival, start at the **Ålesund Aquarium**, located at Tueneset. Open from 10 AM to 5 PM, the aquarium entrance fee is **250 NOK**. It's one of the largest saltwater aquariums in Northern Europe and offers an beautiful experience for visitors of all ages.

For lunch, visit **Racoon Coffee & More** in the city center, known for delicious sandwiches and coffee. Prices range around **150 NOK**, and the café is open from 9 AM to 6 PM.

Spend the afternoon walking up the **418 steps to the Fjellstua viewpoint**, which offers panoramic views of the city and surrounding islands. This activity is free and open year-round, providing a great way to see Ålesund from above.

For dinner, head to **Anno,** a restaurant that specializes in fresh seafood. Meals here range from **300 to 600 NOK** and it's open from 6 PM to 10 PM, providing a cozy dining atmosphere with local ingredients.

You'll spend the night at the **Hotel Brosundet**, offering beautiful water-front views. Rooms start at **1,400 NOK per night**, with check-in at 3 PM and check-out at 12 PM. This hotel is a great base for visiting Ålesund's unique Art Nouveau architecture.

Day 11 Ålesund to Trollstigen

Depart Ålesund in the morning and drive or take a bus to **Trollstigen**, the trip takes about two hours costing around **150 NOK** in fuel. Trollstigen, or the Troll's Path, is a famous mountain road with 11 hairpin bends and incredible views. Spend the morning driving up the road and stopping at the **Trollstigen Visitor Centre**, which is open from 10 AM to 6 PM and has free entry. The center offers beautiful viewpoints and detailed information about the area's geology and a bit of history.

For lunch, you have to bring a packed lunch too or visit the café at the Visitor Centre, where meals cost around **200 NOK**. Spend the afternoon visiting the area, where you can take photos, and possibly hiking some of the nearby trails, which vary in difficulty and length.

Return to Ålesund for dinner the place you may know already at **XL Diner**, famous for its bacalao. The restaurant is open from 5 PM to 10 PM, with dishes costing around **250 to 400 NOK**.

Stay overnight again at **Hotel Brosundet**, with its excellent central location.

Day 12 Ålesund to Jotunheimen National Park

On day twelve, begin the day from Ålesund to **Jotunheimen National Park**. The drive takes about four hours and costs around **300 NOK** in fuel. Alternatively, you can take a bus, which takes about five hours and costs approximately **250 NOK**. Start by visiting the **Jotunheimen Visitor Centre**, located in Lom. The center is open from 9 AM to 5 PM with free entry and provides excellent information about the park and hiking opportunities.

For lunch, visit **Bakeriet i Lom**, known for delicious baked goods and local specialties. Meals cost around **150 NOK**, and the bakery is open from 8 AM to 6 PM.

In the afternoon, hike the **Besseggen Ridge**, one of Norway's most famous hikes as i told you before. The hike is challenging, taking about 6 to 8 hours to complete, and it's recommended for experienced hikers. Make sure that you have good hiking boots, water, and some snacks too. The trailhead is accessible by a ferry from Gjendesheim, costing **150 NOK** one way.

For dinner, you can try the **Fossheim Hotel**, which serves traditional Norwegian dishes. Meals range from **300 to 500 NOK**. The restaurant is open from 6 PM to 9 PM.

Stay overnight at the **Fossheim Hotel**, with rooms starting at **1,200 NOK per night**. The hotel offers comfortable accommodations and is a great base for visiting Jotunheimen National Park.

Day 13 Jotunheimen to Lillehammer

On the thirteenth day, travel from Jotunheimen to **Lillehammer**. If driving, it takes about three hours and costs around **200 NOK** in fuel. Alternatively, take a bus for **150 NOK**, which takes about four hours. Start the day in Lillehammer by visiting the **Maihaugen Open-Air Museum**, located at Maihaugvegen 1. The museum is open from 10 AM to 5 PM with an entrance fee of **150 NOK**. It showcases over 200 historic buildings and offers a fascinating look into Norwegian life through the ages.

For lunch, visit **Heim Gastropub**, which offers a variety of Norwegian and international dishes. Meals cost around **200 NOK**, and the pub is open from 11 AM to 10 PM.

Spend the afternoon exploring the **Lillehammer Art Museum**, which is open from 11 AM to 4 PM with an entry fee of **100 NOK**. The museum features an impressive collection of Norwegian art, from the 19th century to the present day.

For dinner, dine at **Bryggerikjelleren**, known for its fine dining and excellent selection of wines. Meals range from **350 to 600 NOK**. The restaurant is open from 6 PM to 10 PM, offering a refined good dining experience.

Stay overnight at the **Scandic Victoria Lillehammer**, with rooms starting at **1,000 NOK per night**. The hotel is centrally located, making it convenient for further exploration.

Day 14 Lillehammer to Oslo

On your final day, travel from Lillehammer back to **Oslo**. If driving, the trip takes about two hours and costs around **150 NOK** in fuel. Alternatively, take a train for **200 NOK**, which takes about two hours. Once in Oslo, spend your morning visiting the **Munch Museum**, located at Edvard Munchs Plass 1. The museum is open from 10 AM to 6 PM with an entrance fee of **120 NOK**. Here, you can see an extensive collection of Edvard Munch's works, including "The Scream."

For lunch, head to **Mathallen Oslo**, a food hall located at Vulkan 5. The menu include international and Norwegian dishes, with meals costing around **150 to 300 NOK**. The food hall is open from 10 AM to 8 PM.

In the afternoon, take a leisurely walk through **Vigeland Park**, home to over 200 sculptures by Gustav Vigeland. The park is free to enter and open year-round, is a beautiful space to relax.

For dinner, you can have your final meal at **Ekebergrestauranten**, located at Kongsveien 15. This restaurant have beautiful views of the city and serves a variety of gourmet dishes priced between **400 and 800 NOK**. The restaurant is open from 5 PM to 11 PM.

And now, you will end your day and your trip at the **Thon Hotel Opera**, conveniently located near Oslo Central Station. Rooms start at **1,500 NOK per night**, with check-in at 3 PM and check-out at 12 PM. The hotel offers luxurious accommodations and easy access to transportation for your departure.

I hope you enjoied all this activities! Now, i will describe you an alternative themed itinerary's.

CULTURAL TOUR

Day 1 Oslo

You have to start wih **The National Gallery**, at Universitetsgata 13, is a must-see. It's open from 10 AM to 6 PM, and the entry fee is 120 NOK. You'll find famous artworks here, including "The Scream" by Edvard Munch. Then, head to **Akershus Fortress** at Festningsplassen 1. This medieval castle is open from 10 AM to 4 PM and offers incredible views of the harbor. It's free to enter, so you'll get a lot of history for nothing. **The Nobel Peace Center** is another stop, located at Brynjulf Bulls plass 1, open from 10 AM to 6 PM, with a 100 NOK entry fee. This place is full of inspiring exhibits about Nobel Peace Prize laureates and global peace efforts. For the night, **The Thief** at Landgangen 1 is a great place to stay, with rooms starting at 2,500 NOK per night. It's a bit pricey but offers luxury and is close to many attractions. So why not!

Day 2 Bergen

Now, you have to travel to Bergen, either by train or a quick flight. Once there, start at **Bryggen Wharf**, a UNESCO World Heritage Site known for its historic wooden buildings. The shops and cafes here are open from 10 AM to 6 PM. Close by, you'll find **Bergenhus Fortress** at Bergenhus 13, one of Norway's oldest fortifications, open from 10 AM to 4 PM and free to enter. Next, visit the **Hanseatic Museum** at Finnegården 1A, open from 11 AM to 3 PM, with an entry fee of 120 NOK. This museum vividly depicts the life of German merchants during the Hanseatic period. Spend the night at **Clarion Hotel Admiral** at C. Sundts gate 9, with rooms starting at 1,000 NOK per night. For dinner, head to **Enhjørningen** at Bryggen 29, which specializes in traditional cuisine and is open from 4 PM to 10 PM.

Day 3 Stavanger

Now, Travel to Stavanger and go to the **Norwegian Petroleum Museum** at Kjeringholmen 1A. It's open from 10 AM to 5 PM, with an entry fee of 150 NOK. Then, visit **Stavanger Cathedral** at Haakon VIIs gate 2, Norway's oldest cathedral, open from 11 AM to 4 PM, and free to enter. End the day at the **Canning Museum** at Øvre Strandgate 88, open from 10 AM to 4 PM, with an entry fee of 90 NOK. Stay at **Scandic Stavanger City** at Reidar Berges gate 7, with rooms starting at 1,100 NOK per night. For dinner, you can enjoy some sushi at **Sabi Omakase** at Pedersgata 38, open from 5 PM to 10 PM.

ADVENTURE TOUR

Day 1 Tromsø

Kick off your adventure with an exhilarating **dog sledding tour** offered by Tromsø Villmarkssenter. These half-day tours start at 1,500 NOK. In the evening, join a **Northern Lights tour** costing between 900 and 1,500 NOK, starting at 7 PM and lasting around 4-5 hours. For a nice and comfortable stay, you should consider **Radisson Blu Hotel Tromsø** at Sjogata 7, with rooms starting at 1,200 NOK per night. Enjoy a delightful dinner at **Emmas Drømmekjøkken** at Kirkegata 8, open from 5 PM to 10 PM.

Day 2 Lofoten Islands

Take a flight or ferry to the **Lofoten Islands**. Start with a hike up **Reine-bringen**, which offers spectacular views and takes about 2-3 hours round trip. In the afternoon, rent a kayak in Reine for 400 NOK for a half-day to visit the beautiful Reinefjorden. Stay at **Reine Rorbuer**, where is offering a traditional fishermen's cabins with prices starting at 1,800 NOK per night. For dinner, visit **Gammelbua** in Reine, open from 6 PM to 9 PM, for a good local cuisine.

Day 3 Geirangerfjord

Travel to Geirangerfjord and try a **fjord cruise** for 300 NOK for a 1.5-hour tour. Following the cruise, hike to **Skageflå**, an abandoned farm with nice views, which takes about 3-4 hours round trip and requires good fitness. Spend the night at **Hotel Union Geiranger** at Geirangervegen 25, with rooms starting at 1,200 NOK per night. Enjoy dinner at **Brasserie Posten** at Geirangervegen 4, open from 6 PM to 9 PM.

RELAXATION TOUR

Day 1 Oslo

Begin with **Vigeland Park**, open 24/7 and free to enter, featuring over 200 sculptures by Gustav Vigeland. In the afternoon, visit **The Well**, a luxurious spa just outside Oslo, open from 10 AM to 10 PM with an entry fee of 495 NOK. For a beautiful and luxurious stay, book a room at **The Thief**, located at Landgangen 1, with rooms starting at 2,500 NOK per night. For dinner, try **Restaurant Eik** at Universitetsgata 11, open from 5 PM to 10 PM.

Day 2 Sognefjord

Go to the Sognefjord and enjoy a **floating sauna** in Flåm, priced at 350 NOK per person, open from 10 AM to 6 PM. In the afternoon, take a **Sogne-fjord cruise**, where is starting at 300 NOK. Stay at **Fretheim Hotel**, located at Flam 5743, with rooms priced at 1,200 NOK per night. For dinner, visit **Ægir Brewpub**, known for its Viking-style atmosphere and craft beers, located at Flåmsbrygga, open from 6 PM to 10 PM.

Day 3 Hardangerfjord

Visit a fruit farm in **Hardangerfjord** for 200 NOK to enjoy fresh local produce. Stay at **Ullensvang Hotel**, with rooms starting at 1,500 NOK per night, where is offering luxurious amenities and beautiful views. Check-in is at 3 PM, and check-out is at 11 AM. For Dinner go at **Glacier Restaurant**, located at Lofthus 5781, known for its beautiful views and local ingredients, open from 6 PM to 9 PM.

CURATED ITINERARIES

3-DAY ITINERARY MUST-SEE ATTRACTIONS AND ACTIVITIES

Day 1 Oslo

You're going to start in **Oslo**. Then head to the **National Gallery** at Universitetsgata 13, open from 10 AM to 6 PM, with an entry fee of 120 NOK. Next, visit **Akershus Fortress** at Festningsplassen 1, open from 10 AM to 4 PM and free to enter. End the day at the **Nobel Peace Center** at Brynjulf Bulls plass 1, open from 10 AM to 6 PM, entry 100 NOK. Stay at the **Radisson Blu Scandinavia Hotel**, located at Holbergs gate 30, with rooms starting at 1,200 NOK per night. For dinner, try **Fiskeriet Youngstorget** at Youngstorget 2B, known for its seafood, open from 11 AM to 10 PM.

Day 2 Bergen

Go to the Bergen and visit the **Bryggen Wharf**, open from 10 AM to 6 PM, free entry. Visit the **Bergenhus Fortress**, open from 10 AM to 4 PM, free entry. Visit the **Hanseatic Museum**, open from 11 AM to 3 PM, entry 120 NOK. You can stay at the **Clarion Hotel Admiral**, located at C. Sundts gate 9, with rooms starting at 1,000 NOK per night. Then, for dinner you should try **Enhjørningen** at Bryggen 29, where is known for traditional Norwegian cuisine, open from 4 PM to 10 PM.

Day 3 Stavanger

Visit the **Norwegian Petroleum Museum**, open from 10 AM to 5 PM, entry 150 NOK. Visit **Stavanger Cathedral**, open from 11 AM to 4 PM, free entry. End at the **Canning Museum**, open from 10 AM to 4 PM, entry 90 NOK. Stay at the **Scandic Stavanger City**, located at Reidar Berges gate 7, with rooms starting at 1,100 NOK per night. For dinner, try **Sabi Omakase** at Pedersgata 38, known for its sushi, open from 5 PM to 10 PM.

Day 4 Geirangerfjord

Take a **fjord cruise** for 300 NOK, available throughout the day. Hike to **Skageflå**, which takes about 3-4 hours round trip, and is free to visit. Stay at the **Hotel Union Geiranger**, located at Geirangervegen 25, with rooms starting at 1,200 NOK per night. For dinner, visit **Brasserie Posten** at Geirangervegen 4, open from 6 PM to 9 PM.

Day 5 Ålesund

Visit the **Atlanterhavsparken Aquarium**, open from 10 AM to 4 PM, entry 200 NOK. Climb up to **Aksla Viewpoint**, free and open all day. Go at the **Art Nouveau Center**, open from 10 AM to 5 PM, entry 100 NOK. You can stay at **Hotel Brosundet**, where is located at Apotekergata 5, with beautiful rooms starting at 1,300 NOK per night. For dinner, try the famous **XL Diner**, known for its bacalao, located at Skaregata 1B, open from 5 PM to 10 PM.

Day 6 Trondheim

Visit the **Nidaros Cathedral**, open from 9 AM to 2 PM, entry 120 NOK. Explore **Kristiansten Fortress**, free entry, open from 9 AM to 9 PM. Visit the **Ringve Music Museum**, open from 11 AM to 4 PM, entry 100 NOK. Stay at the **Scandic Nidelven**, located at Havnegata 1-4, with rooms starting at 1,200 NOK per night. For dinner, visit **To Rom og Kjøkken**, known for local menu, located at Carl Johans gate 5, open from 5 PM to 10 PM.

Day 7 Kristiansand

Start with **Kristiansand Zoo and Amusement Park**, open from 10 AM to 5 PM, entry 500 NOK. Visit the **Posebyen**, the old town, free to walk around. See the **Agder Museum of Natural History and Botanical Garden**, open from 10 AM to 4 PM, entry 100 NOK. Stay at the **Radisson Blu Caledonien Hotel**, located at Vestre Strandgate 7, with rooms starting at 1,000 NOK per night. For dinner, try **Mother India**, located at Markens gate 6, known for its Indian cuisine, open from 5 PM to 10 PM.

Day 8 Alta

Travel to Alta and then visit the **Alta Museum**, open from 10 AM to 5 PM, entry 100 NOK. See the **Northern Lights Cathedral**, open from 11 AM to 3 PM, free entry. Stay at **Scandic Alta**, where is located at Løkkeveien 61, with small rooms starting at 1,000 NOK per night. For dinner, you have to try the **Restaurant Haldde**, where is located at Markveien 38, open from 6 PM to 9 PM.

Day 9 Kirkenes

Check the **Snowhotel**, open for tours from 12 PM to 4 PM, entry 200 NOK. Take a **king crab safari**, priced at 1,500 NOK. Stay at **Thon Hotel Kirkenes**, where located at Johan Knudtzens gate 11, with rooms starting at 1,200 NOK per night. For dinner, try **Thon Hotel Restaurant**.

Day 10 Svalbard

Fly to Svalbard. Visit the Longyearbyen. See the **Svalbard Museum**, open from 10 AM to 5 PM, entry 100 NOK. Stay at **Radisson Blu Polar Hotel Spitsbergen**, with rooms starting at 2,000 NOK per night. For dinner, try **Huset** in Longyearbyen, open from 6 PM to 10 PM.

Day 11 Back to Oslo

Now, you have to return to Oslo. You can spend the day at leisure or revisit any missed attractions. Stay at **The Thief**, located at Landgangen 1, with rooms starting at 2,500 NOK per night. For dinner, try **Restaurant Eik**, located at Universitetsgata 11, open from 5 PM to 10 PM.

Day 12 Oslo Surroundings

Take a day trip to **Holmenkollen Ski Museum**, open from 10 AM to 4 PM, entry 140 NOK. Visit **Viking Ship Museum**, open from 10 AM to 4 PM, entry 120 NOK. Return to Oslo for dinner at **Maaemo**, located at Dronning Eufemias gate 23, open from 5 PM to 10 PM.

Day 13 Day Trip to Drøbak

Go to the Drøbak and visit the **Oscarsborg Fortress**, is open from 10 AM to 6 PM, entry 100 NOK. Check the **Tregaardens Julehus**, the year-round Christmas shop, open from 10 AM to 5 PM. Then, return to Oslo and stay at **The Thief**. For dinner, try **Dinner Bar & Restaurant**, located at Stortingsgata 22, open from 5 PM to 11 PM.

Your last day

Spend your last day visiting any remaining sights or enjoying some last-minute shopping before heading back to home.

SELECTED EXCITING DAY TRIPS

VISIT THE DRØBAK IN OSLO

You'll love a day trip to Drøbak, a beautiful coastal town offering a nice combination of the history and culture. **Start by taking the bus from Oslo Bus Terminal**; the ride is about an hour and costs around **100 NOK**. Once you arrive, go straight to **Oscarsborg Fortress**, an beautiful historic site located on a small island in the Oslofjord. To get there, **take a short ferry ride from the Drøbak pier**, costing **70 NOK** for a round trip. **The fortress is open daily from 10 AM to 6 PM**, and the entry fee is **100 NOK**. Here, you can see the history of the fortress, visiting museums, and have beautiful views of the fjord.

After your visit to the fortress, go to the Tregaardens Julehus, the year-round Christmas shop that brings festive cheer no matter the season. Where is located in the middle of Drøbak, it's open from **10 AM to 5 PM** and offers a good shopping experience with a wide array of Christmas decorations and gifts. For lunch, I recommend you the **Galleri Café Teskje**, where is situated at Niels Carlsens gate 4. This cozy café, open from **11 AM to 5 PM**, serves delicious sandwiches, cakes, and hot beverages, making it a great spot to relax and people-watch.

Next, visit the Drøbak Aquarium at Havnebakken 6, showcasing the rich marine life of the Oslofjord. The aquarium is open from **10 AM to 5 PM**, and the entry fee is **90 NOK**. It's an engaging place to learn about local sea creatures. **End your day with a leisurely stroll along the charming streets of Drøbak**, lined with picturesque wooden houses and gardens. And for art, as you may know already, the **Drøbak Art Gallery** is worth a visit, featuring works by local artists and open from **12 PM to 6 PM**.

DAY TRIP FROM BERGEN

The Flåm and the Aurlandsfjord
  Let's start from Bergen to Flåm, a quaint village nestled in the Aurlands-

fjord, renowned for its spectacular beauty. **Begin your visit by taking the Bergen Railway to Myrdal**, then switch to the world-famous Flåm Railway. The entire trip takes about 2.5 hours, and a round-trip ticket costs around **800 NOK**. Upon arriving in Flåm, one of the highlights is a **fjord cruise on the Aurlandsfjord**. Cruises depart regularly from the Flåm Marina and cost approximately **300 NOK** for a 1.5-hour trip. **The waters and dramatic cliffs are wonderful.**

After the cruise, visit the Flåm Railway Museum, conveniently located next to the train station. Open from **9 AM to 6 PM** with free entry, the museum offers insights into the engineering marvel of the Flåm Railway and the region's history. For lunch, head to **Ægir BrewPub** at Flåmsbrygga. This Viking-inspired pub, open from **11 AM to 10 PM**, is famous for its craft beers and good meals.

In the afternoon, if you're up for a short hike, the trail to Brekkefossen offers wonderful views of the valley and fjord. The trailhead is just a 15-minute walk from the center of Flåm, and the hike itself is moderate, taking about 1.5 hours round trip. Alternatively, if you are more adventure oriented, a **RIB boat tour** provides a good way to visit the fjord's inlets and waterfalls, priced at around **600 NOK**.

DAY TRIP FROM STAVANGER

VISIT PULPIT ROCK (PREIKESTOLEN)

A trip to Pulpit Rock (Preikestolen) is a must when you're in Stavanger. Start with a ferry ride from Stavanger to Tau, which takes about 40 minutes and costs **60 NOK** each way. From Tau, a bus will take you to the Preikestolen trailhead, a 20-minute trip costing **50 NOK**. The hike to Pulpit Rock is approximately 4 hours round trip, covering 8 kilometers with some steep sections. **The panoramic views from the top**, with a sheer drop into the Lysefjord below, are simply incredible. You have to wear sturdy hiking boots and pack water and some snacks. **There are no entry fees for the hike, and it's open year-round, though the best time to visit is from May to September for the safest conditions.**

After your hike, head back to Stavanger and treat yourself to a well-deserved dinner at Flor & Fjære, a beautiful garden restaurant located at

Skagenkaien 35-37. Open from **6 PM to 10 PM**, this nice dining amidst lush gardens is a must.

DAY TRIP FROM TROMSØ

Visit the Lyngen Alps

For a day trip from Tromsø, go to the majestic Lyngen Alps. Begin by taking a ferry from Breivikeidet to Svensby, a 20-minute ride costing **50 NOK**. The Lyngen Alps offer some of the most incredible peaks and best hiking opportunities in the region. One popular hike is to **Blåvatnet (Blue Lake)**, a moderate 3-hour round trip hike that leads to a mesmerizing turquoise glacial lake. The trailhead is located about a 1-hour drive from Svensby, and the hike itself offers panoramic views of the surrounding mountains and valleys.

Now, you can end your trip by going back in Tromsø with a nice meal at Mathallen, located at Grønnegata 58-60, open from **5 PM to 10 PM**. Their menu have Arctic specialties.

13 FEATURES AND INSIGHTS

EXTRAORDINARY EXPERIENCES

Booking a **Northern Lights safari** is one of the best things you can do. **To book a tour, you have to check out operators like Chasing Lights, Tromsø Safari, and Arctic Explorers.** You can book on their websites, through travel agencies, or even after you arrive in places like Tromsø. **Prices usually range from 1,200 to 2,500 NOK per person** depending on what the tour includes, like meals, warm clothes, or photography services.

When you go on a **Northern Lights safari**, you'll be taken to areas far from city lights to see the aurora. **Tours usually last 4-7 hours, starting around 6 PM and going late into the night.** The tour guides provide thermal suits, boots, and sometimes hand and foot warmers. **You have to wear layers of clothes, with thermal underwear, warm sweaters, and a windproof and waterproof outer layer.** Also a hat, gloves, and a scarf to keep warm is a good idea.

Some of the best places for a **Northern Lights safari** are Tromsø, the Lofoten Islands, and Svalbard. **You can fly to Tromsø from Oslo in about 2 hours or take a coastal ferry with Hurtigruten.** For the Lofoten Islands, fly into Svolvær or take a ferry from Bodø. Svalbard is more remote and reachable by flying from Oslo or Tromsø.

The best time to see the Northern Lights is from late September to early April, with peak viewing from December to February. First, **check the aurora forecast and weather conditions before your trip.** Clear, dark skies are essential, and Tromsø is a great spot for sightings. **Tour operators like Chasing Lights and Tromsø Safari give regular updates and will reschedule tours to improve your chances of seeing the aurora.**

Tour operators like **Chasing Lights and Tromsø Safari** offer many services. Their packages usually include transportation to the best viewing spots, experienced guides, thermal clothing, and sometimes professional photographers. **Chasing Lights offers a "Small Group Aurora Chase" that includes minibus transportation, warm overalls, boots, hot beverages, and tripods for photography.** Prices are usually around 1,500 to 2,000 NOK per person.

For a good experience, you may want to stay in an **Aurora Camp**. These camps are set up in perfect viewing locations and often include traditional Sami tents (lavvu) for overnight stays. **Tromsø Lapland and Green Gold of Norway** offer these experiences.

I suggest you to plan the trip between late September and early April for the best chance to see the Northern Lights. **Most tours start around 6 PM and can last until midnight or later, depending on the aurora activity.** During the peak season (December to February), book your tour early to ensure a spot.

VIKING HERITAGE TOURS

Start at the Viking Ship Museum in Oslo, where you'll be amazed by the well-preserved Oseberg, Gokstad, and Tune ships. **Located on the Bygdøy peninsula,** you can get there by taking bus number 30 from Oslo city center, which takes about 20 minutes. **The museum is open daily from 9 AM to 6 PM in summer and from 10 AM to 4 PM in winter.** Entrance fees are 120 NOK for adults and free for children under 18. **You'll see a lot of Viking artifacts, like carved sleds, tools, and household items, showing what life was like in the Viking age.**

Next, head to the **Lofotr Viking Museum in Borg, in the Lofoten Islands.**

This museum is built around the largest Viking longhouse ever found, giving you a full look at Viking life. **Interactive exhibits and reenactments bring the Viking era to life.** The museum is open from 10 AM to 5 PM in summer and from 10 AM to 3 PM in winter, with an entry fee of 200 NOK for adults and 100 NOK for children. **You can drive or take a bus from Svolvær, which takes about an hour.** Participate in activities like boat rowing, axe throwing, and enjoying traditional Viking feasts.

Then, visit **Njardarheimr Viking Village in Gudvangen,** where you can do activities like archery, axe throwing, and join workshops on Viking crafts. **It's open daily from 10 AM to 6 PM, with admission at 190 NOK for adults and 120 NOK for children. Take a bus or drive from Bergen, about a two-hour trip.** This village lets you experience Viking life firsthand, with weaving, blacksmithing, and storytelling around the fire.

In **Stiklestad, the Stiklestad National Cultural Center** brings the important Battle of Stiklestad in 1030 to life with detailed exhibits and reenactments. **The center is open from 10 AM to 4 PM, with an entrance fee of 150 NOK for adults and 75 NOK for children. Reach it by train and bus from Trondheim, a two-hour journey.** This site is important for understanding the Christianization of Norway and its impact on Viking culture.

Don't miss the annual Viking Festival in Hafrsfjord, near Stavanger, held every June. This festival features battle reenactments, market stalls, and Viking music and food. **Reach Hafrsfjord by bus from Stavanger, a 30-minute journey, with festival admission around 150 NOK for adults.** The festival shows Viking life with artisans demonstrating crafts like leatherworking, woodworking, and blacksmithing.

For accommodations, you have to **consider the luxurious Thief Hotel in Oslo,** offering rooms starting at 2,500 NOK per night. It's close to the Viking Ship Museum and has great views of the Oslofjord. In Lofoten, **the Nyvågar Rorbuhotell in Kabelvåg** offers traditional cabins starting at 1,800 NOK per night, enhancing your historical experience with the feel of Viking seafaring life.

For dining, try Frognerseteren Restaurant near the Viking Ship Museum in Oslo, where you can enjoy traditional Norwegian dishes like reindeer steak and klippfisk (dried and salted cod) with amazing views of the Oslofjord. In Lofoten, **Børsen Spiseri in Svolvær** serves fresh seafood and local specialties such as stockfish and Lofoten lamb, giving you a taste of the region's rich culinary heritage.

ACTIVITIES UNDER THE MIDNIGHT SUN

The Midnight Sun in Norway is really a special thing. In the summer, above the Arctic Circle, the sun doesn't set. This creates a unique opportunity for many activities.

Hiking is a favorite during this time. With the sun always up, you can take longer hikes that might be hard to finish in one day. A great hike is the Reinebringen Hike in Lofoten. You can get to the starting point by traveling to the village of Reine. First, take a ferry from Bodø to Moskenes, then a short bus ride. The hike is steep and tough but offers amazing views of the islands, especially under the Midnight Sun. Bring water and wear good hiking boots because the trail is challenging.

If you prefer water activities, boating under the Midnight Sun is very peaceful. You can book a boat trip from Tromsø and sail on the calm fjord waters. Companies like Arctic Adventures offer midnight kayaking tours. These usually start around 10 PM and end early in the morning. You'll paddle while the sun stays low on the horizon. These tours cost between 800 and 1,200 NOK and often include equipment and a light meal.

Cultural events and festivals are also unique during this time. In Tromsø, the Sami Week in June celebrates the culture of the indigenous Sami people. The festival includes music, dance, and craft markets. Events start in the afternoon and go late into the night. Most are free, but some might have a small fee.

Adjusting to the continuous daylight can be tough, but it means you can enjoy activities whenever you want. To help adjust, use blackout curtains where you stay and keep a regular sleep schedule. When outside, you may need to wear sunglasses to protect your eyes from the bright sun.

For places to stay, look for accommodations that help you enjoy the Midnight Sun with minimal effort. The Scandic Ishavshotel in Tromsø has rooms with blackout curtains and is close to the harbor, making it easy to join late-night trips. Rooms start at about 1,500 NOK per night. If you want a rustic experience, stay in rorbu cabins in Lofoten. These cozy fishermen's cabins cost around 1,000 to 1,500 NOK per night, depending on the location and amenities.

For dining, choose restaurants open late so you can enjoy a meal while it's still light outside. Fiskekompaniet in Tromsø is a good choice. It's known for fresh seafood and great waterfront views. They serve until midnight during summer, with main dishes costing between 200 and 400 NOK.

14 PHRASES

GREETINGS AND POLITENESS

s essential to know how to greet people and express basic politeness in a new country. Knowing a few words can make a big difference in your interactions and how warmly people receive you. So, start with some basics like **"Hei"** (hi), pronounced **"Hi"**, or if you want to be a bit more formal, use **"Hallo"** (hah-loh), which means hello. For different times of the day, you can say **"God morgen"** (goo mohr-gen) for good morning, **"God dag"** (goo dahg) for good day, **"God kveld"** (goo kvel) for good evening, and **"God natt"** (goo naht) for good night. When you want to be polite, **"Vær så snill"** (vaer so snill) means please, and **"Takk"** (tahk) is thank you. If you need to express even more gratitude, you can say **"Tusen takk"** (too-sen tahk), meaning thank you very much. And, when someone thanks you, it's nice to reply with **"Ingen årsak"** (in-gen or-sahk), which means you're welcome. If you need to get someone's attention or apologize, **"Unnskyld meg"** (oon-shild my) is the way to say excuse me.

ASKING FOR HELP AND DIRECTIONS

If you need to ask about prices, say **"Hvor mye koster dette?"** (voor mee-eh kost-er deh-teh) which means how much does this cost? If you're looking for a restroom, ask **"Hvor er toalettet?"** (voor air toh-ah-let-et) where is the bathroom? Communication can be easier if you ask **"Snakker du engelsk?"** (snak-er doo eng-elsk), which means do you speak English? In case you get lost, saying **"Jeg har gått meg vill"** (yai har got my vil) meaning I am lost, can be very helpful. If you need assistance, ask **"Kan du hjelpe meg?"** (kan doo yelp-eh my) can you help me? For finding a pharmacy, say **"Hvor er nærmeste apotek?"** (voor air naer-mes-teh ah-po-tek), which means where is the nearest pharmacy?

DINING OUT

When you dine out, it's useful to know how to ask for what you need. Well, If you need the menu, ask **"Kan jeg få menyen, vær så snill?"** (kan yai fo men-yen, vaer so snill), meaning can I have the menu, please? When you're ready for the bill, say **"Kan jeg få regningen, vær så snill?"** (kan yai fo reg-ning-en, vaer so snill) can I have the bill, please? If you have allergies, it's crucial to communicate that, so say **"Jeg er allergisk mot..."** (yai air al-er-gisk mot) I am allergic to… If you prefer vegetarian food, ask **"Har dere vegetarretter?"** (har deh-reh veh-get-ar-ret-er) do you have vegetarian dishes? For recommendations, say **"Hva anbefaler du?"** (vah an-beh-fah-ler doo) what do you recommend? And if you simply need water, ask **"Kan jeg få vann, vær så snill?"** (kan yai fo vann, vaer so snill), which means can I have water, please?

TRANSPORTATION

To ask how to get somewhere, say **"Hvordan kommer jeg meg til...?"** (vordan kom-mer yai my til) how do I get to...? If you need to know the bus schedule, ask **"Når går bussen?"** (nor gor boos-en) when does the bus leave? To find the nearest bus stop, say **"Hvor er nærmeste bussholdeplass?"** (voor air naer-mes-teh boos-hold-eh-plahs) where is the nearest bus stop? To find out the cost of travel, ask **"Hvor mye koster en billett til...?"** (voor mee-eh kost-er en bil-let til) how much is a ticket to...? And if you're curious about travel time, say **"Hvor lang tid tar det å komme dit?"** (voor lang teed tar deh å kom-meh deet) how long does it take to get there?

SHOPPING

If you want to try something on, say **"Kan jeg prøve denne?"** (kan yai pruh-veh den-neh) can I try this on? If you need a different size, ask **"Har dere denne i en annen størrelse?"** (har deh-reh den-neh ee en an-nen stoer-rel-seh) do you have this in another size? To check if you can use your card, say **"Godtar dere kredittkort?"** (god-tar deh-reh kred-itt-kort) do you accept credit cards? And always get a receipt by saying **"Kan jeg få en kvittering?"** (kan yai fo en kveet-eh-ring) can I get a receipt?

EMERGENCIES

Emergencies can be stressful, but knowing what to say can be important. When you need urgent help (i hope not!), shout **"Hjelp!"** (yelp) which means help! If you need a doctor, say **"Jeg trenger en lege"** (yai tren-ger en leh-geh) I need a doctor. To call the police, ask **"Kan du ringe politiet?"** (kan doo ring-eh poh-lee-teet) can you call the police? If you've lost your passport, say **"Jeg har mistet passet mitt"** (yai har mis-tet pahs-seh mitt) I have lost my passport. If you feel unwell, say **"Jeg føler meg dårlig"** (yai foel-er my dor-lig) I feel sick.

CULTURAL CUSTOMS

To ask how to greet people, say **"Hvordan hilser jeg?"** (vor-dan hil-ser yai) how do I greet? If you want to know if taking photos is allowed, ask **"Er det greit å ta bilder her?"** (air deh greit å tah bil-der hair) is it okay to take photos here? For restaurant recommendations, say **"Kan du anbefale en god restaurant?"** (kan doo an-beh-fah-leh en goo res-taw-rant) can you recommend a good restaurant? To understand local customs better, ask **"Er det noen spesielle skikker jeg bør vite om?"** (air deh noo-en spe-si-ell-eh shik-er yai bør vee-teh om) are there any special customs I should know about?

COMMUNICATION TIPS

In Norway, directness and honesty are highly valued in communication, so it's best to say what you mean clearly and respectfully. Locals are generally reserved, which means small talk might not come easily, but once you start a conversation, they are usually friendly and open. When it comes to gestures and body language, people prefer to maintain a bit of distance while talking since personal space is important. A firm handshake is the typical greeting, and keeping eye contact shows you're paying attention, but don't overdo it because staring can seem rude. Nodding while someone is speaking indicates that you are actively listening.

In conversations, people speak calmly, and it's considered rude to interrupt, so always wait until the person has finished talking before you respond. Avoid sensitive topics like politics or personal income unless you know the person well. Instead, focus on subjects like the outdoors, local traditions, or sports like skiing. Compliments are appreciated, but make sure they are genuine and not overdone.

Respect is a key aspect of the culture. For instance, when you visit someone's home, always take off your shoes at the door. If you're invited to a meal, bring a small gift like flowers or chocolates as a token of appreciation. Wait until everyone is served before you start eating, and at the end of the meal, it's polite to say "takk for maten" (tahk for mah-ten), which means thank you for the food. People typically use utensils for most foods, even items you might eat with your hands elsewhere.

Certain phrases and gestures should be avoided to prevent misunderstandings. While a thumbs up is usually positive, pointing with your finger can be seen as rude. Avoid swearing or using very informal language unless you are close with the person. Exaggerated compliments can seem insincere, so keep your praise simple and genuine. Additionally, try to avoid making loud noises in public, as it's considered disruptive.

Effective communication means matching the style of the person you're talking to. If they're formal, maintain formality; if they're casual, you can relax your tone as well. Always listen actively and nod to show you understand. If you don't understand something, ask for clarification rather than guessing. For example, in a café, a polite wave can get the waiter's attention; don't shout or make loud noises.

Locals might seem reserved at first, but they are warm and welcoming once you get to know them. Look for non-verbal cues like facial expressions and body language to understand how they feel. If someone speaks softly or avoids eye contact, they might be shy. Matching their tone and demeanor can make them feel more comfortable. A genuine smile can also help bridge cultural gaps and create a positive interaction.

LEARNING RESOURCES

Learning Norwegian can be really fun and rewarding, especially when you have the right resources to help you along the way. First, you should definitely try **Duolingo**. It's a fantastic app that's free and very user-friendly, breaking the language into small, manageable lessons, so you'll learn vocabulary and basic grammar through short exercises. Another great app is **Babbel**, which focuses more on practical conversation skills, and although it's subscription-based, it offers in-depth lessons that help you speak Norwegian in real-life situations.

If you like books, you might want to check out **"Norwegian in 10 Minutes a Day" by Kristine Kershul** because this book breaks down the language into easy chunks and includes exercises to help you practice. Another excellent book is **"Teach Yourself Complete Norwegian" by Margaretha Danbolt-Simons** since this one comes with an audio CD, which is very helpful for mastering pronunciation.

If you prefer online courses, the **University of Oslo** offers a free course called **"Introduction to Norwegian"**. It's perfect for beginners and covers the basics in a structured way. Another good option is **Memrise**, an online platform that offers various Norwegian courses created by both users and experts, focusing on vocabulary and phrases, using spaced repetition to help you remember what you've learned.

One of the best ways to improve your language skills is by practicing with locals. If you're in Norway, don't be shy about starting conversations in Norwegian, because most people will appreciate your effort and be happy to help. **Language exchange programs like Tandem** allow you to connect with native speakers who want to learn your language, so this mutual exchange is a fantastic way to practice speaking regularly.

Setting realistic goals is crucial for staying motivated. Start with small, achievable targets like learning ten new words a day or practicing speaking for five minutes daily, and as you become more comfortable, you can gradually increase your goals. Keeping a journal of new words and phrases you've learned can be very motivating since you can see how much you've improved over time.

Staying motivated can sometimes be challenging, but making learning fun can help. Watch Norwegian TV shows or movies with subtitles to get used to the sounds of the language and improve your listening skills, and listening to Norwegian music or podcasts while you're on the go can also be very beneficial. Joining a language learning community, either online or in person, can provide support and encouragement. Websites like **Reddit's r/Norwegian** or various language forums are great for asking questions, sharing tips, and connecting with other learners.

Local language schools in Norway offer courses for all levels. For example, **Folkeuniversitetet** has campuses in several cities and offers a range of Norwegian courses, and **Oslo Voksenopplæring** provides courses specifically designed for immigrants and international students. These schools provide a structured learning environment and the opportunity to practice with other learners.

Useful websites include **NorskNet**, which offers interactive exercises and lessons, and **Loecsen**, which provides basic vocabulary and phrases with audio pronunciations, so these resources can supplement your learning and offer different ways to practice. You will thank me!

15 APPENDICES

TOURIST INFORMATION CENTERS

Checking the tourist information centers in Norway can be really helpful.

Well, In **Oslo**, go to the **Oslo Visitor Centre** at Jernbanetorget 1, inside the Oslo Central Station. It's open every day from 9 AM to 6 PM. There you can get maps, brochures, and personalized advice here. Call them at +47 23 10 62 00 or check their website for more info. If you're arriving by train, it's super convenient as it's right inside the station. This center also offers free Wi-Fi, luggage storage services, and the Oslo Pass, which gives you access to numerous attractions and public transport.

In **Bergen**, visit the **Bergen Tourist Information Centre** at Strandkaien 3. They're open from 8:30 AM to 4:30 PM on weekdays and from 9 AM to 2 PM on weekends. They can help you plan your visit to the fjords or explore the city. Contact them at +47 55 55 20 00 or look online for more details. Located by the Fish Market, it's easy to reach by bus or by foot from most central hotels. The center also has lockers for storing your belongings, sells Bergen Cards for free or discounted entry to attractions, and offers detailed walking maps.

Up in **Tromsø**, stop by the **Tromsø Tourist Information Centre** at

Kirkegata 2. It's open from 9 AM to 5 PM on weekdays and from 10 AM to 3 PM on weekends. They can give you tips on seeing the Northern Lights and other winter activities. Call them at +47 77 61 00 00 or visit their website for more info. It's close to the main bus stops, making it easy to reach. They provide weather updates, crucial for planning Northern Lights trips, and also offer booking services for local tours and activities.

For the fjords, the **Geiranger Tourist Information Centre** at Maråkvegen 35 is great. It's open from 9 AM to 6 PM in the summer. They have guides for hiking and boat tours. Reach them at +47 70 26 30 99. It's right by the harbor, perfect if you're arriving by ferry. They offer detailed hiking maps, can book tours, and provide real-time information about road conditions and weather, which is essential for planning safe trips in the fjord area.

In **Stavanger**, the **Stavanger Tourist Information Centre** at Domkirke-plassen 3 is the place to go. It's open from 9 AM to 5 PM on weekdays and from 10 AM to 4 PM on weekends. They can help you plan your hike to Pulpit Rock or explore the city. Contact them at +47 51 85 92 00 or find more info online. Located near the Stavanger Cathedral, it's easy to find and reach by public transport. They offer tickets for local attractions and public transport passes, and you can also rent bicycles here.

These centers are really useful. They offer useful local **maps**, **brochures**, and lots of **local tips**. You can find out about events, good places to eat, and hidden gems. Many centers have apps or websites with up-to-date info, so you can use those too. Most of these centers also offer services like booking accommodation, tickets for local events, and detailed guides for hiking or driving routes.

EMERGENCY NUMBERS

For any emergency, dial **112**. This connects you to the local police, fire, and ambulance services. When calling, be ready to provide your location, the nature of the emergency, and your contact details. Speak clearly and stay calm. This is a 24/7 service, and the operators speak English.

If you need medical assistance but it's not a life-threatening emergency, dial **113** for medical services. They will ask for details about your condition, your location, and any relevant medical history. Be clear about your symptoms and follow their instructions carefully. If you're unsure whether your situation is an emergency, it's better to call.

For the police, if you need non-emergency assistance, dial **02800**. This is useful for reporting minor incidents or seeking advice. You'll need to provide your location and the nature of your concern. They can guide you on what steps to take next.

If you lose your passport or need assistance from your home country's embassy, here are a few key contacts:

- **U.S. Embassy in Oslo:** Call +47 21 30 85 40. Located at Morgedalsvegen 36, it's open Monday to Friday from 8 AM to 4:30 PM. They can help with lost passports, legal issues, and emergencies involving U.S. citizens.
- **British Embassy in Oslo:** Call +47 23 13 27 00. Located at Thomas Heftyes gate 8, it's open Monday to Friday from 9 AM to 4 PM. They provide similar services for British nationals.
- **Canadian Embassy in Oslo:** Call +47 22 99 53 00.

Located at Wergelandsveien 7, they're open Monday to Friday from 8:30 AM to 4:30 PM. Assistance includes passport services, legal help, and emergency situations.

For tourists, the **112 Norge** app is highly recommended. It allows you to contact emergency services with your GPS location automatically sent to responders, ensuring they can find you quickly even if you're unsure of your exact location.

EMBASSIES AND CONSULATES

The U.S. Embassy is situated in Oslo at Morgedalsvegen 36. Should you need to contact them, you can dial +47 21 30 85 40. They provide various services, including visa assistance, passport renewals, and emergency support. If you need to visit the embassy, ensure you bring your passport and any other necessary documents. Moreover, it's advisable to book an appointment online to minimize waiting time and ensure you receive the help you need efficiently.

Similarly, the British Embassy, which is also located in Oslo, can be found at Thomas Heftyes gate 8. You can reach them at +47 23 13 27 00. This embassy offers support for lost or stolen passports, legal advice, and assistance during emergencies. In case of an urgent situation, call them and clearly explain what's happening. Remember to bring your passport and any relevant paperwork to facilitate the process.

For Canadian citizens, the embassy is located at Wergelandsveien 7 in Oslo. Their contact number is +47 22 99 53 00. Services offered include passport renewals and visa applications. In case of emergencies, you should call the embassy with your identification and details of the issue. Booking an appointment online beforehand can make your visit smoother.

The Australian Embassy that covers Norway is located in Copenhagen at Dampfærgevej 26. You can contact them at +45 70 26 36 76. They assist with visas, passports, and emergency situations as well. If you require help, call them to explain your situation. It's best to check their website for appointment bookings and necessary documents to bring along.

For French nationals, their embassy is in Oslo at Drammensveien 69. Their phone number is +47 23 28 46 00. They offer services such as passport renewals, visa processing, and emergency support. In case of an emergency, call them with your details ready. Scheduling an appointment online is recommended, and make sure to bring your passport and any required documents.

CONCLUSION

We reached the end of this basic but very informative guide, you have to know that I've put a lot of effort into making this manual as complete and useful as possible, providing you almost a Norway comprehensive resource for your trip. **I sincerely hope that you have found almost everything you need**, helping you feel well-prepared and excited.

As you may know already, the travel conditions and information can change frequently, so **it's will be important to keep updating yourself about all the relevant details you may need before planning the vacation**. Staying informed through sources such as travel blogs, social media platforms, and other online information can enhance the amount of information you need to feel safe. These platforms often provide real-time updates and also some personal insights that can be incredibly useful. Thank you and hope we will meet one time in Norway!

Made in the USA
Monee, IL
12 January 2025

76662913R00072